Voices of the Chicago Eight
A Generation On Trial

Voices of the Chicago Eight
A Generation On Trial

BY TOM HAYDEN, RON SOSSI, FRANK CONDON

With court transcripts featuring
Abbie Hoffman, Bobby Seale, Jerry Rubin, Rennie Davis,
Dave Dellinger, John Froines, Tom Hayden, Lee Weiner

City Lights Books
San Francisco

Cover design: Pollen

Text design: Gambrinus

Library of Congress Cataloging-in-Publication Data

Sossi, Ron.
  [Chicago conspiracy trial]
  Voices of the Chicago eight : a generation on trial / by Tom Hayden, Frank Condon, Ron Sossi.
      p. cm.
  "With court transcripts featuring Abbie Hoffman, Bobby Seale, Jerry Rubin, Rennie Davis, Dave Dellinger, John Froines, Tom Hayden, Lee Weiner."
  Includes the complete play "The Chicago conspiracy trial" by Ron Sossi and Frank Condon, along with an introduction and three additional essays by Tom Hayden.
      ISBN 978-0-87286-495-5 (pbk.)
      1. Chicago Seven Trial, Chicago, Ill., 1969–1970—Drama. 2. Trials (Conspiracy)—Illinois—Chicago—Drama. 3. Riots—Illinois—Chicago-—History. I. Condon, Frank. II. Hayden, Tom. III. Title. IV. Title: Voices of the Chicago 8.

PS3569.O717C47 2008
812'.54—dc22

City Lights Books are published at the City Lights Bookstore,
261 Columbus Avenue, San Francisco, CA 94133.
Visit our Web site: www.citylights.com

Special thanks to Lynn Damme for making "The Chicago Conspiracy Trial" fit seamlessly into this volume.

CONTENTS

THE CONSPIRACY LIVES

by Tom Hayden

The trial of the Chicago Eight encapsulated the politics and counter-culture of the1960s. Reading the texts that document the events and give voice to the witnesses and defendants, one gets a full sense of the mix of the confrontation, creativity, openness, militancy, and spontaneity that defined the era and drove the trial. Focus of testimony went far beyond what happened in the streets of Chicago during the 1968 Democratic Convention. Attention also focused on the significance of other movement moments: Selma, Berkeley, Columbia University, the Pentagon, People's Park. Our witnesses recalled our history. Timothy Leary and Allen Ginsberg relived the be-ins; Cora Weiss read a letter from a survivor of Song My; Julian Bond described the violence of the South and the funeral of Martin Luther King. The testimony traced our gradual development as revolutionaries: Bobby Seale, a comedian, GI, mechanic, community worker, then a Black Panther; Rennie Davis, a chicken judger, basketball star, student government leader, founder of Students for a Democratic Society (SDS), community organizer and peace activist; Abbie Hoffman, a graduate psychology student, civil rights worker in North and South, organizer of a peace candidate's campaign, then a dropout on the Lower East

Side—six of us who came alive in the Beat Generation, former graduate students, civil rights workers, peace marchers, and campaign workers. We had been building a movement for ten years. It felt like all of that movement was on trial and we were the scapegoats.

This feeling was confirmed when we spoke around the country, meeting thousands of young people who felt themselves to be part of the ordeal. They read about the trial in the underground and overground press; it was a surreal theater in which the whole country seemed to be cast.

Forty years later, the voices of Chicago 1968 continue to resonate. Zbigniew Brzezinski called the student rebellions of that year "the death rattles of the historical irrelevants." Brett Morgan's critically acclaimed documentary *The Chicago 10* was released earlier this year, and Steven Spielberg may follow with a major film working from a script written by Aaron Sorkin. Tom Brokaw's history of the sixties is a bestseller, and *Newsweek* already has published a cover story. These are likely only previews of things to come as the fiftieth anniversary of the 1960s approaches in 2010.

A superficial explanation for all the attention is that the media likes round numbers. Anniversaries propel them to produce commemorative pieces. But that alone doesn't account for the production of so many movies, books, and magazine specials, all looking back.

A deeper explanation is that there's an ongoing battle over history and memory. Social movements like those that mobilized the antiwar protests of the 1960s first arise unnoticed, then go through the tear gas of police and flash of cameras, and then get carried with their bruises into the mainstream where a majority reluctantly, gradually, but steadily, supports their cause. When the Vietnam antiwar movement won, however, the triumph was disguised as the Establishment's victory, as Kissinger's peace prize. The fight continues, however, over how it all is—and will be—remembered.

There are three typical approaches to this battle over memory. First, there are those who never change. Vietnam, they say, was a noble war and the protesters nothing but treasonous long-haired youth. Second are those who manage history for purposes of maintaining their status and power. Ending the Vietnam War by congressional action and freeing the Chicago conspirators by an appellate court decision, they say, only proved that the System worked. Finally, there are those like myself or Howard Zinn who believe credit should go to the radicals who, in every age, take a stand against injustice whatever the price to their liberties, and struggle to force concessions from those with power.

The fight over memory is important to each generation's perception of their possibilities. Claiming that order was restored by the courts or that the System itself has restorative powers undermines a sense of agency and empowerment for new generations wondering how they can make a difference.

How the 1960s are remembered is even deeply entangled in the presidential contest now underway between senators John McCain, Hillary Clinton and Barack Obama. McCain's fighter-bomber was blown out of the sky over Hanoi in October 1967, the very week of the Pentagon demonstrations that foreshadowed Chicago. Hillary Clinton was there in the streets of Chicago for three nights, though she claims she was only a witness. Barack Obama makes a powerful appeal to "turn the page" from 1960s' dramas to a "new generation of leadership," but he still stands on the Selma bridge to display himself as a successor to those who came before.

This City Lights book is a resource for anyone interested in exploring the undercurrents of 1968 still flowing through our cultural and political arteries today. The dramatic rendition of the trial by Ron Sossi and Frank Condon is based on the verbatim transcripts of what was said and done in the courtroom. The chapters on Chicago—from the streets to the trial to the verdict—represent the history of Chicago events from my experience.

City Lights and its founder, poet Lawrence Ferlinghetti, the original publishers of *Howl*, are highly appropriate publishers for this account of American history. Allen Ginsberg's poetry and presence helped launch the Beat Generation of the 1950s and counterculture of the 1960s which ultimately transformed American culture. Allen Ginsberg was one of the few established figures who braved the wrath and gas of the Chicago police in 1968 and became a central witness in the Chicago trial.

It is helpful to lay down a brief timeline for understanding the sequence of events concerning Chicago:

- August 25–28, 1968: the week of street confrontations coinciding with the Democratic National Convention;

- September 1968: Democratic Attorney General Ramsey Clark declines to prosecute the case;

- March 20, 1969: Republican Attorney General John Mitchell announces federal indictment;

- September 24, 1969: trial begins under auspices of Judge Julius Hoffman;

- November 3, 1969: Bobby Seale chained and gagged; mistrial declared November 5;

- February 20, 1970: jury finds five defendants guilty of incitement, not guilty of conspiracy; bail is denied; John Froines and Lee Weiner found innocent on both counts;

- February 28, 1970: U.S. Seventh Circuit Court of Appeals overturns bail ruling; defendants freed on bail;

- May 11, 1972: U.S. Seventh Circuit reverses contempt citations; U.S. government decides to retry contempt citations;

- November 21, 1972: U.S. Seventh Circuit reverses federal convictions;

- October 30, 1973: retrial on 154 contempt citations begins under Federal Justice Edward Gignoux;

- December 5, 1973: Gignoux rules 146 contempt citations invalid, finds Kunstler, Dellinger, Rubin and Hoffman guilty of total fourteen citations; defendants are sentenced to time served.

Now consider the events that shaped the conspiracy trial during those same five years, a convulsion unknown since the Civil War:

- The assassinations of Martin Luther King on April 4, 1968, and Robert Kennedy on June 5, 1968;

- The riots after King's murder, April, 1968;

- Columbia University strike, along with hundreds of other campuses, April 1968;

- President Johnson's pledge to resign, March 31, 1968;

- The Soviet invasion of Czechoslovakia, August 1968;

- Nixon's law-and-order campaigns and his secret police plan;

- Nixon's election by 0.4 percent, November 1968;

- State troopers' killing of James Rector and blinding of Alan Blanchard in People's Park, May 15, 1969;

- Apollo 11 astronauts Neil Armstrong and Buzz Aldrin becoming the first humans to walk on the moon, July 20, 1969;

- Sharon Tate murdered by Charles Manson gang, August 9, 1969;

- Woodstock Festival, August 15–18, 1969;

- My Lai massacre exposed, William Calley charged, September 5, 1969;

- Vietnam Moratorium, October 15, 1969;

- Chicago police killing of Black Panthers Fred Hampton and Mark Clark, December 4, 1969;

- Earth Day, April 22, 1970;

- Three members of the Weather Underground die in accidental explosion while building bombs in a Greenwich Village townhouse, March 6, 1970;

- President Nixon orders the U.S. invasion of Cambodia, April 30, 1970;

- National student strike called at Yale, May 1, 1970, hundreds of campuses closed;

- National Guardsmen kill four students, wound nine others, at Kent State, May 4, 1970;

- Troopers kill two students at Jackson State, May 15, 1970;

- Reformers take over Democratic Party in primaries and convention, July 1972;

- President Nixon reelected over McGovern, November, 1972;

- Watergate hearings begin, May 1972;

- Nixon forced to resign the presidency, August, 1973; Congress begins cutting funds for war.

If the two columns are woven together, one begins to get a sense of what we went through during those explosive five years.

Approached this way, the events surrounding the trial of the Chicago Eight seem to be a passion play—staged first in the streets and later in a courtroom—that evoke all the dramas of the 1960s concentrated in one place.

Our lives were being churned by a larger storm. Love, death, war, peace, social change and experimentation, everything was magnified, accelerated. Anything seemed possible. Millions marched and danced, organized almost spontaneously: Woodstock, Moratorium, Earth Day, student strikes, the McGovern campaign, the forced resignations of presidents. And just as uncontrollably, our elders and movement comrades, presidents and potential presidents, were assassinated one by one.

Behind the cascade of individual events, the thread is the collapse of the Cold War State, with its military anticommunism abroad and enforced obedience at home. The decade began under the pall of conformist ethos, McCarthyism and censorship of the 1950s, and ended in the rout of a Nixon law-and-order administration only a few years later. The turning point, I believe, came in the aftermath of the Chicago trial. On the day of our conviction, hundreds of protests and riots exploded on campuses across the country, most visibly in the burning of a Bank of America branch in Isla Vista. Within months, Nixon's invasion of Cambodia and the killings at Kent State had provoked far greater outrage. Rennie Davis led a tumultuous Washington protest that May, and in the eyes of the establishment the country seemed to be falling apart. The president's own Commission on Campus Unrest reported in 1970 that "the crisis on American campuses has no parallel in the history of the nation, and this crisis has roots in divisions in American society as deep as any since the Civil War." Borrowing from the rhetoric of the 1962 *Port Huron Statement*, the report even asked for understanding of the new emerging lifestyles of young, "manifested by differences in dress and lifestyle." The report asserted that nothing was more important than ending the war in Indochina. The authors went on to conclude,

"If this trend continues, if this crisis of understanding endures, the very survival of the nation will be threatened. A nation driven to use the weapons of war upon its youth is on the edge of chaos. A nation that has lost the allegiance of part of its youth is a nation that has lost a part of its future."

The Commission's report followed the reasoning of an earlier, secretive, and arguably illegal report by the Central Intelligence Agency to the president, called "Restless Youth," dated September 4, 1968—one week after the Chicago convention demonstrations. Forwarded by CIA Director Richard Helms to Presidential Assistant Walt Rostow, the report diagnosed the youth revolt as a global one against faceless and insensitive institutions. The CIA rejected the view that the revolt was Communist inspired, instigated, funded or controlled. On the contrary, the CIA found mass unrest among youth, even in the Soviet Union.

Slowly and surely, then, the American establishment began backing away from the posture of imperial confrontation toward one of rapprochement with forces that could not be defeated. The most important but least-mentioned reason usually given for why the sixties "ended" is simply this: on issue after issue, the efforts of sixties' radicalism prevailed. By this I do not mean that sixties radicals individually succeeded, nor that the radical visions that grew from the confrontations succeeded, but that the core issues ultimately found support from a majority of Americans. Examples:

- in response to mass movement efforts, civil disobedience and protest, the war in Vietnam was ended and the draft was abolished;

- in response to student organizing, 18-year-olds won the right to vote and campus curricula were profoundly reformed;

- where before there were smoke-filled rooms, now the presidential primaries were open and women comprised half the delegates to the Democratic conventions;

- in response to Earth Day, the administration passed the strongest package of environmental laws in the nation's history;

- in response to repression, the first reforms of the FBI and CIA were enacted since the beginning of the Cold War.

When the core demands of mass movements appear to be achieved, people tend to refocus on their everyday lives. And so the epic and spontaneous turmoil of the 1960s subsided as substantial reforms were won during early 1970s.

The government could have decided to retry the Chicago conspiracy defendants, but chose not to. The law under which we were tried—the so-called "Rap Brown law" prohibiting interstate travel for the purpose of inciting to riot—has never been used again by any prosecutors anywhere.

The threat of a national police state decreased. The Vietnam War ended and President Carter declared an amnesty for 50,000 American "deserters" in Canada.

As the achievements of the 1960s were absorbed and mellowed by the mainstream, some of us didn't see the backlash coming. The presidencies of Ronald Reagan and George Bush were aggressive countermovements aimed at overturning what they called "the Vietnam Syndrome" of the 1960s.

The culture and memory war to diminish and trivialize the sixties continues to this day. Even the generally affirmative history by Tom Brokaw is entitled *Boom!*, as in "boomers," a demographic term which sixties-era activists refuse to be reduced to. We of the sixties generation never could completely triumph, not after the assassinations of the Kennedys and King, but neither will the sixties ethos be defeated, because the norms of the sixties have become too deeply entrenched in American culture and politics, and reminders are always with us, from Katrina to Baghdad.

There is a final reason why the voices of the Chicago Eight continue to resonate today. It is because the U.S. wars in Iraq and Afghanistan and the policies of the Bush administration awaken memories of the past and call us out from complacency. It is not enough to sing Beatles songs when an illegal war is being waged again, when the reasons for war are being fabricated again, when dissent is being called unpatriotic again, when American firepower is being used against Third World farmers and villagers again, when resources for education and health care are being siphoned away for war again, and when another environment is being ravaged in the pursuit of oil.

It is time for a new generation to get angry and question our government once again, before it is too late. That generation is powerfully manifest in the grassroots support in 2008 for Barack Obama, a force that I have not seen since the Robert Kennedy campaign of 1968.

The time of the Chicago Eight is passing away. Dave Dellinger, Abbie Hoffman, Jerry Rubin, Bill Kunstler, and our appellate attorney, Arthur Kinoy, have passed on. Rennie Davis is an entrepreneur in Colorado, John Froines a public health professor in Los Angeles, Lee Weiner worked for the Anti-Defamation League (last I heard). Bobby Seale keeps the Black Panther history and legacy alive in Oakland and online. My close friend Len Weinglass still soldiers on in the courts, now with international human rights cases. As for me, the stages of life move on with uncomfortable speed. Eight years ago I retired from twenty years in California politics. Now I teach and write about yet another war, and find myself spending considerable time answering questions about the sixties.

All I can say, looking back, is that we somehow found the spirit in ourselves to take a stand against repression, fear and silence, because we felt we had to. Wherever our words or deeds are welcome in this generation, it is gratifying to know that conspiracies can thwart the power of prosecutors, and live beyond their graves in memory and history.

—Tom Hayden
Los Angeles
May 1, 2008

Antiwar demonstrators rally in support of the Chicago Eight, spring 1969. NACIO JAN BROWN

I.

The Chicago Conspiracy Trial

A Play by Ron Sossi and Frank Condon

With court transcripts featuring Abbie Hoffman, Bobby
Seale, Jerry Rubin, Rennie Davis, Dave Dellinger, John
Froines, Tom Hayden, Lee Weiner

DIRECTOR'S NOTE

by Frank Condon

I was walking through the student center at U.C. Santa Barbara one day in 1969, as the trial was raging, when I came upon a group of theater students reading portions of the trial transcripts out loud. A crowd had gathered, and I found it compelling; I thought then that it would make a helluva play in about ten years. It would document an extremely important event in American history and be a powerful piece of political theatre. Nearly a decade later, in 1978, I met with Ron Sossi at the Odyssey Theater in Los Angeles. Ron said he ran across a reference to the Chicago conspiracy trial, and that it might make a exciting evening of theater. Ron asked if I was interested in working with him on a theatrical adaptation of the transcripts of the trial. I, of course, jumped at it, and we immediately went to work obtaining and poring over transcripts. We soon had a storyboard set up in Ron's office, and there were pieces of scenes all over my living room carpet, ready to be Scotch-taped together. I went into rehearsal while Ron and I were still working on major elements of the play, and I was trying sections out with the actors to see how they worked—or didn't. Leonard Weinglass was helping one night in rehearsal, and he said something about how the actual trial was so boring, but the play was exciting. I told him that Ron and I simply took out all the boring parts.

The Chicago conspiracy trial lasted more than five months. We have, of course, condensed the transcripts for this docudrama representation of the event. Every word, however, is taken directly from the transcripts of the trial. The only exceptions are that some of the government witnesses' names have been changed, because in certain cases testimony has been combined for structural unity. Also, purely for structural reasons, the chronology of some events has been rearranged. The final script evolved during weeks of trying out and keeping or eliminating portions of the transcripts during the course of rehearsals.

The Chicago Conspiracy Trial was first produced at the Odyssey Theatre, Los Angeles, on March 6, 1979, with the following cast.

JUDGE JULIUS HOFFMAN	George Murdock
DAVID DELLINGER, *defendant*	Logan Ramsey
RENNIE DAVIS, *defendant*	Dan Mason
TOM HAYDEN, *defendant*	Lance Rosen
ABBIE HOFFMAN, *defendant*	Paul Lieber
JERRY RUBIN, *defendant*	Karl Gregory Clemens
LEE WEINER, *defendant*	Lonnie Ellison
JOHN FROINES, *defendant*	John Ellis
BOBBY SEALE, *defendant*	Leopoldo Mandeville
WILLIAM M. KUNSTLER, *defense*	Lev Mailer
LEONARD WEINGLASS, *defense*	Kenneth Tigar
STU BALL, *defense*	Stan Roth
THOMAS AQUINAS FORAN, *prosecution*	Hal Bokar
RICHARD G. SCHULTZ, *prosecution*	Tom Bower
KRISTI A. KING, *juror*	Dena Lesser
RUTH L. BILLINGSLEY, *juror*	Joan Blair
DAVID E. STAHL, *witness*	John Christy Ewing
SGT. BAILEY/MAYOR DALEY, *witnesses*	Marty Davis
BARBARA BRADDOCK, *witness*	D. J. Sydney
R. CONNELLY/R. PETERSON, *witnesses*	John Darrah
WILLIAM ALBRIGHT, *witness*	John W. Davis
R. GRANDHOLM/J. B. HATLEN, *witnesses*	Robert Alan Browne

ALLEN GINSBERG, *witness*	Hal Schwartz
MICHELLE DELLINGER, *spectator*	Martina Fink
JEFF MILLER, *spectator*	Steve Tracy
SHARON, *Weiner's girlfriend*	Robin Ginsburg
SUSAN, *Davis's girlfriend*	Janice Galloway Dow
TOM GRACE, *spectator*	Arye Gross/Ed Levey
U.S. MARSHAL RON DOBROWSKI	Kenneth Dobbs
SEALE'S CUSTODIAN	Randy Johnson
COURT REPORTER	Lou Hancock
MARSHALS	John Sammon, David Watkins, Joshua Cadman

Directed by Frank Condon
Produced by Ron Sossi

SETTING

The United States Courthouse, Chicago, Illinois, September 1969 through February 1970

ACT ONE

No. 69 CRIM. -180 United States of America Plaintiff

v.

David T. Dellinger, Rennard C. Davis, Thomas E. Hayden
Abbott H. Hoffman, Jerry C. Rubin, Lee Weiner, John R. Froines and
Bobby G. Seale, Defendants

SCENE ONE
United States District Court
Chicago, Illinois
September 26,1969

CLERK: Will all please rise. (*Enter* JUDGE HOFFMAN.) The United States District Court for the Northern District of Illinois is now in session. The Honorable Julius J. Hoffman presiding. Please be seated. No. 69 CR 180 United States of America versus David T. Dellinger, et al. Case on trial.

COURT: Mr. Marshal, will you please bring in the jury.

Blackout.

SCENE TWO

Opening Statements

September 26, 1969

MR. SCHULTZ: Ladies and gentlemen of the jury, Mr. Foran, counsel for the defendants. The Government will prove that each of the eight defendants in this case conspired together to encourage people to riot during the Democratic National Convention, which was held in Chicago from August 26 through August 29, 1968. We will prove, ladies and gentlemen of the jury, that the defendant David Dellinger, who sits right there, and the defendant Rennard Davis, who sits next to him, and Thomas Hayden, who is standing, that these three men . . .

COURT: Who is the last defendant you named?

SCHULTZ: Mr. Hayden.

COURT: The one that shook his fist in the direction of the jury?

HAYDEN: That is my customary greeting, Your Honor.

COURT: It may be your customary greeting, but we do not allow shaking of fists in this courtroom.

HAYDEN: It implied no disrespect for the jury; it is my customary greeting.

COURT: Regardless of what it implies, sir, there will be no fist shaking and I caution you not to repeat it. That applies to all the defendants. Mr. Schultz.

SCHULTZ: In promoting and encouraging this riot, the three men whom I just mentioned used an organization, which they called the National Mobilization Committee to End the War in Vietnam, to plan these activities. Two of these defendants, the defendant Abbie Hoffman, who sits—who is just standing for you, ladies and gentlemen . . .

COURT: The jury is directed to disregard the kiss thrown by the defendant Hoffman and the defendant is directed not to do that sort of thing again.

SCHULTZ: . . . and with them a man named Jerry Rubin who is standing there—these two men called themselves leaders of the Yippies.

HOFFMAN AND RUBIN: Yippie!

COURT: Contempt of court is any act calculated to hinder or disrupt the Court in its administration of justice. Mr. Schultz.

SCHULTZ: Two more of these individuals—Lee Weener, who is a research . . .

WEINER: Weiner.

SCHULTZ: . . . Lee Weiner, who just stood, who is a research assistant—calls himself a professor of sociology at Northwestern University, and John Froines . . . He is an assistant professor of chemistry at the University of Oregon. Weener and Froines joined . . .

WEINER: Weiner.

SCHULTZ: . . . joined with Davis, Dellinger, and Hayden. And the eighth person who joined is a man named Bobby Seale, seated at the end of the table. Ladies and gentlemen of the jury, we will prove that each of these eight men assumed specific roles, and that the plans to incite the riot were basically in three steps. The first step was to use the unpopularity of the war in Vietnam as a method to urge people to come to Chicago during that convention for purposes of protest. The second step was to incite these people against the police department, the city officials, the National Guard, and the military, and against the convention itself, so that these people would physically resist and defy the orders of the police and the military. The third step was to create a situation where the demonstrators who had come to Chicago and were conditioned physically to resist the police, would meet and would confront the police in the streets of Chicago so that at the confrontation a riot would occur.

In sum then, ladies and gentlemen, the Government will prove that the eight defendants charged here conspired together to use the facilities of interstate commerce to incite and further a riot in Chicago; that they conspired to use incendiary devices to further that riot, they conspired to have people interfere with law enforcement officers, and that the defendants committed overt acts in the furtherance of this conspiracy. Ladies and gentlemen of the jury, the Government will prove each of these eight defendants guilty as charged.

COURT: Is it the desire of any lawyer of a defendant to make an opening statement?

KUNSTLER: It is, Your Honor.

COURT: All right. You may proceed, Mr. Kunstler.

KUNSTLER: Ladies and gentlemen of the jury. We hope to prove before you that this prosecution that you are hearing is the result of two motives on the part of the Government . . .

SCHULTZ: Objection as to any motives of the Prosecution, if the Court please.

KUNSTLER: Your Honor, it is a proper defense to show motive.

COURT: I sustain the objection. You may speak of the guilt or innocence of your clients, not to the motive of the Government.

KUNSTLER: Your Honor, I have always thought that . . .

SCHULTZ: Objection to any colloquies and arguments, Your Honor.

COURT: I sustain the objection, regardless of what you have always thought, Mr. Kunstler.

KUNSTLER: The Defense will show that the real conspiracy in this case is the conspiracy to curtail and prevent the demonstrations against the war in Vietnam and related issues; that these defendants and other people, thousands, who came here were determined to influence the delegates of a political party meeting in Chicago; that the real conspiracy was against these defendants. But we are going to show that the real conspiracy is not against these defendants as individuals, because they are unimportant as individuals. The real attempt was—the real attack was on the rights of everybody, all of us American citizens, all, to protest against a war that was brutalizing, is brutalizing, us all, and to protest in a meaningful fashion. And that the determination was made that the protest would be dissolved in the blood of the protesters; that the protest would die in the streets of Chicago; and that the protest would be dissipated and nullified by police officers under the guise of protecting property, or protecting law and order, or protecting other people. Dissent died here for a moment during that Democratic National Convention. What will happen in this case will decide whether it is dead.

SCHULTZ: Objection, Your Honor.

COURT: I sustain the objection. I direct the jury to disregard the last statement of counsel for the defendants. Does any other defense lawyer wish to make an opening statement? Just a minute, sir, who is your lawyer?

SEALE: Charles R. Garry.

COURT: Mr. Kunstler, do you represent Mr. Seale?

KUNSTLER: No, Your Honor, as far as Mr. Seale had indicated to me, that because of the absence of Charles R. Garry due to surgery . . .

COURT: Have you filed his appearance?

KUNSTLER: Filed whose appearance?

COURT: The appearance for Mr. Seale.

KUNSTLER: I have filed an appearance for Mr. Seale.

COURT: All right. I will permit you to make another opening statement in behalf of Mr. Seale, if you like. I will not permit him to address the jury.

KUNSTLER: Your Honor, I cannot compromise Mr. Seale's position . . .

COURT: I don't ask you to compromise it, sir, but I will not permit him to address the jury with his very competent lawyer present here.

KUNSTLER: I want the record to indicate quite clearly that I do not direct Mr. Seale in any way. He is a free, independent black man who does his own direction.

COURT: What an extraordinary statement, "an independent black man." He is a defendant in this case. He will be calling you a racist before you are through, Mr. Kunstler.

KUNSTLER: Your Honor, I think to call him a free, independent black man will not incite his anger.

Blackout.

SCENE THREE
Case for the Prosecution
September 30, 1969

FORAN: Your Honor, we apologize for being late this morning, but before you bring in the jury . . . We were just contacted by the FBI. It seems that one of the jurors had received a letter, or her family had received a letter, that certainly could be of a threatening nature. I have a copy of it here, Your Honor, marked Government's Exhibit A. It is addressed to the King family.

COURT: Now, my own marshal, gentlemen, was handed this communication addressed to the Billingsley family. It is not unlike

Government's Exhibit A. Mr. Marshal, will you please go to the jury room and request Juror Kristi A. King and Juror Ruth L. Billingsley to accompany you to the courtroom one at a time?

KUNSTLER: Your Honor, we move to have an evidentiary hearing.

FORAN: The Government objects to . . .

COURT: The objection is sustained. The motion is denied. You are Miss, is it, Kristi A. King?

KING: Yes.

COURT: Miss King, the marshal has handed you Government's Exhibit A for identification. Will you please look at that document and tell me whether you have ever seen it before.

KING: No, sir, I haven't.

COURT: You have never seen it?

KING: No, sir.

COURT: Do you know whether any member of your family brought it to your attention or not?

KING: No one ever brought it to my attention, no, sir.

COURT: Read it, Miss King. Just read it, please.

KING: "You are being watched. The Black Panthers." And it is addressed to the King family.

COURT: Now having seen that document, do you feel that you can remain a fair and impartial juror in this case?

KING: No, sir.

COURT: What did you say?

KING: No, sir.

KUNSTLER: Your Honor, I must make an objection for the record. This juror had never seen this letter before Your Honor showed it to her. The most minimal investigation by the Federal Bureau of Investigation would have revealed from her father and mother that she had not seen it. I think it was Your Honor's duty to discontinue questioning in this case, because now the Court has revealed the letter.

COURT: The objections of the Government will be sustained and the motion denied. Under the circumstances I have no alternative, since the juror has said that having seen this letter, she cannot function fairly and impartially as a juror. You are excused from further service, Miss King. Mr. Marshal, let me have the first alternate juror's card.

KUNSTLER: Your Honor, I think the interrogation should go further here. She should be questioned as to her knowledge of the Panthers, what they are, what her thoughts are, and so on.

COURT: The Panthers aren't indicted here, sir. I am not trying the Panthers. I know nothing about them.

SEALE: But I am a member of the Panther Party.

KUNSTLER: We think they are indicted, Your Honor, in the eyes of the public.

COURT: Mr. Marshal, will you please instruct that defendant to remain quiet during this discussion.

WEINGLASS: If the Court please, may I just be heard on a point of law with respect to this matter. The United States Supreme Court has recently handed down . . .

COURT: I will not interrogate this juror as to her knowledge of this— what do they call it—the Black Panthers, if indeed such an organization exists—and I don't know whether it does. I am not trying any organization here; I am trying eight individuals.

WEINGLASS: Your Honor . . .

COURT: A juror has the right to say he or she can't be fair. Alternate juror Kay Richards will be substituted for juror Kristi A. King. You are Ruth L. Billingsley?

MRS. BILLINGSLEY: Yes.

COURT: The marshal is handing you Government's Exhibit B-2 for identification. Will you please tell the court whether or not you have ever seen this before?

MRS. BILLINGSLEY: Yes. We received this in the mail—when was it? Monday.

COURT: When you say "we," you mean your family?

MRS. BILLINGSLEY: My family, yes.

COURT: Having seen that letter, do you still feel that you can continue to be a fair and impartial juror?

MRS. BILLINGSLEY: Yes.

COURT: And that you can give these eight defendants as well as the United States of America . . .

MRS. BILLINGSLEY: Yes, I do.

COURT: . . . a fair and impartial trial?

MRS. BILLINGSLEY: Yes.

COURT: You do?

MRS. BILLINGSLEY: Yes. I think it is my duty to.

COURT: This juror will be permitted to remain on the jury.

KUNSTLER: Your Honor, the defendants believe the two letters in question were sent by some agent of the Government in order to prejudice them further in this trial.

COURT: I will let you try to prove that right now. That is a very grave charge against an officer of the Government.

KUNSTLER: Well, we obviously can't prove it, Your Honor.

COURT: Then don't say it.

KUNSTLER: That is my clients' position. That is my statement.

COURT: To make a statement like that is irresponsible.

KUNSTLER: We would hope that Your Honor would set this down for a hearing, so that what Your Honor has termed—and we agree with Your Honor—is a very serious allegation can at last begin to unravel in this courtroom.

FORAN: Your Honor, the Government objects to the totally frivolous, idiotic proposal that you have hearings to determine inferences of possibilities of circumstantial evidence. I wish really—well, Your Honor, the Government objects to it. It is so—I wish the showboat tactics would stop.

COURT: Mr. Marshal, I direct you at an appropriate time after this hearing to see to it that the members of the jury are sequestered, and that the newspapers and other journals and radio and television are kept from them, and any other people who might try to talk with them.

KUNSTLER: Your Honor, the Defense moves for the un-sequestration of the jury. We think it is more humane.

COURT: I will deny the motion. Assuming there is such a word as— what did you call it?

KUNSTLER: I said "un-sequestration," Your Honor. We mean that they should not be locked up during the trial.

COURT: I have treated your motion as such.

CLERK: There is a motion here of defendant Bobby Seale *pro se* to be permitted to defend himself.

COURT: I will hear you, Mr. Seale.

SEALE: I, Bobby Seale, demand and move the Court as follows. Because I am denied the lawyer of my choice, Charles R. Garry, I cannot represent myself as my attorney would be doing. Because I am forced to be my own counsel and to defend myself, I require my release from custody, from the bail presently in force, so that I can interview witnesses, do the necessary factual research, and all the other things being in custody makes impossible, including the right to cross-examine witnesses and examine witnesses of my choice. I know we've gotten some attack from the Government saying that we're playing games over here, but I'm not playing no games with my life being stuck on the line, and I want to put that in the record to explain my situation.

COURT: Have you finished, sir?

SEALE: Yes.

COURT: All right.

SCHULTZ: May we briefly reply, Your Honor?

COURT: Mr. Schultz.

SCHULTZ: Your Honor, this is a ploy. It's just a simple, obvious ploy. The defendants know perfectly well that if Mr. Seale were to cross-examine witnesses here and argue to the jury we would have a mistrial in this case in two minutes. There is absolutely no doubt about that. He would destroy the defendants' right to a fair trial. They know that, and they know perfectly well, him not being a lawyer, there would be reversible error and there would be nothing we could do about it.

COURT: I shall order the longhand document filed. It is signed not "Bobby Seale, Defendant" but in the manner: "Bobby Seale, Chairman, Black Panther Party." I know of no such designation in the pleadings in this case. However, I shall treat the document as a motion of the defendant's. I find now that to allow the defendant Seale to act as his own attorney would produce a disruptive effect.

SEALE: Disruptive!

COURT: The complexity of the case makes self-representation inappropriate, and the motion of the defendant will be denied.

Blackout.

SCENE FOUR
Testimony of Government Witness DAVID E. STAHL
Deputy Mayor of Chicago

FORAN: Thank you, Mr. Stahl. Now, will you now point Mr. Hoffman and Mr. Rubin out to the jury.

STAHL: Yes. Mr. Hoffman just stood up and waved his hand. Mr. Rubin is sitting there in a yellow-striped polo shirt.

FORAN: Thank you.

COURT: Will you cross-examine, Mr. Kunstler?

KUNSTLER: Yes, Your Honor. Now, in all your discussions with either Jerry Rubin, Abbie Hoffman, Dave Dellinger, Rennie Davis, or any of the people with them, did anyone ever say to you, "If we don't get the permits, we're going to do violent acts in this city"?

STAHL: Not in precisely that language, no.

KUNSTLER: Well, did they say it in any language?

STAHL: Yes, Mr. Dellinger said during the Monday meeting that permits for the use of parks should be issued in order to minimize destruction.

KUNSTLER: To minimize destruction. And did he indicate to you from whence this destruction would come?

STAHL: It certainly wasn't coming from the Chicago Police Department. (*Laughter from* DEFENDANTS.)

KUNSTLER: Are you serious? Is this a serious answer?

FORAN: Oh, come on, now. He is in this argumentative fashion trying to play Perry Mason.

KUNSTLER: He does pretty well, Your Honor. If I could do half as well as Perry Mason . . .

FORAN: As a television actor, you do, Mr. Kunstler.

COURT: Mr. Marshal, I will ask you to maintain order out there.

KUNSTLER: Your Honor, a bit of laughter is not disorder, and I think sometimes . . .

COURT: It is in this courtroom. This is either a serious case or it isn't. I don't waste my time. Now, Mr. Weinruss . . .

WEINGLASS: Weinglass, Your Honor.

COURT: Mr. Weinglass.

WEINGLASS: Mr. Stahl, about the permit process. Now, in your August 7th meeting where you testified that Abbie and Jerry . . .

FORAN: Your Honor, here we go again. Now another man in his 30s being called "Abbie Baby." I object to the diminutive, familiar, child terms for mentally grown men.

KUNSTLER: Your Honor, I did not hear "Abbie Baby."

WEINGLASS: "Abbie Baby?"

FORAN: "Abbie and Jerry." I mean this is foolishness.

KUNSTLER: I object to that, Your Honor.

COURT: I sustain the objection of the Government.

KUNSTLER: Would Your Honor order the jury to disregard the "Abbie Baby" remark as unfounded?

COURT: If the United States Attorney said that, I certainly will. Crowd the "baby" out of your minds. We are not dealing with babies here. Please continue Mr. . . .

WEINGLASS: Weinglass, Your Honor. At the August 7th meeting with Abbie Hoffman and Jerry Rubin, did Mr. Hoffman and Mr. Rubin indicate to you that if the Yippies were permitted to stay in the park that everything would be OK and nonviolent?

STAHL: I don't recall words exactly to that effect being—or statements to that effect being made at that meeting.

WEINGLASS: What was the general tenor of their remarks, Mr. Stahl?

STAHL: They opened the meeting by saying they wanted to avoid violence. They also followed that statement subsequently with statements about their willingness to tear up the town and the convention, and to die in Lincoln Park.

WEINGLASS: But in between that first statement you made and the second, did they not indicate that if the city would permit them to stay in the parks, that there would be no violence and that everything would be all right?

STAHL: I would suspect they made a statement something along those lines in the course of the meeting.

WEINGLASS: Thank you. I am showing you your handwritten notes of the August 12th meeting, marked Defendants' Exhibit 8. Is that your handwritten note, a copy of it?

STAHL: Yes, these are a copy of my notes of the meeting on August 12th.

WEINGLASS: Directing your attention to the first page, did you state right at the beginning that the National Mobilization Committee made it clear to you at the outset that they wanted to avoid unnecessary tensions? Is that correct?

STAHL: Mr. Dellinger made that statement and immediately followed with a statement that he believed in civil disobedience, that he just returned from Paris where he studied police riots. I think that he would say violence and then nonviolence and then say . . .

WEINGLASS: Is that correct? Well, does that statement appear in your notes?

STAHL: Yes, the statement about civil disobedience does.

WEINGLASS: Yes, now would you read to the jury, after having said that, what your notes reflect Mr. Dellinger said about civil disobedience?

FORAN: Object to that.

COURT: I sustain the objection.

WEINGLASS: Is it not a fact that Mr. Dellinger said that he believes in civil disobedience, but that he does not intend to disrupt delegates to the convention? Isn't that what he said, Mr. Stahl? Isn't that what your notes reflect him saying?

FORAN: Your Honor, I object to that.

COURT: I sustain the objection.

WEINGLASS: I ask you to look over that entire first page, and I ask you whether or not there are any notations indicating that Mr. Dellinger had been to Paris or that he had studied riot techniques on that first page?

FORAN: Your Honor, I object to this. There is clearly a proper way to establish that if it is true.

COURT: Of course, I sustain your objection.

WEINGLASS: Do you further recall Mr. Dellinger saying to you in the course of that meeting that he didn't want to interfere with the police, business, or traffic? I am referring to page two of your notes.

STAHL: Yes, he made that statement.

WEINGLASS: He made that statement. Did he also make a statement to you that he wanted to meet with the police?

STAHL: He said he *may* want to meet with the police.

WEINGLASS: I refer you to the middle of the page. Does it qualify—does he say he wants to meet with the police?

STAHL: My notes say, "Wants to meet with the police."

WEINGLASS: Yes. Did Mr. Dellinger also make known to you, as reflected in your notes, that a denial of permits is a denial of rights?

STAHL: Yes.

WEINGLASS: Thank you, Mr. Stahl.

COURT: Is there any redirect examination?

SCHULTZ: Yes, Your Honor. Now Mr. Stahl . . .

SEALE: *(Quietly.)* I would like to cross-examine the witness.

COURT: You may not cross-examine, sir.

SEALE: Well, I think I have the right to cross-examine.

COURT: You have a lawyer here.

SEALE: He is not my lawyer. That is not true. I made the choice of Charles R. Garry to represent me.

KUNSTLER: May I say I have withdrawn or attempted to withdraw.

MARSHAL: Mr. Seale, will you sit down.

SEALE: I want my rights. I want my right to defend myself in this trial. I want my rights recognized.

COURT: Now, you just keep on this way Mr. Seale, and . . .

SEALE: Keep on what? Keep on what? Keep on getting denied my constitutional rights?

COURT: Will you be quiet?

SEALE: You think black people don't have a mind. Well, we got big minds, good minds, and we know how to come forth with constitutional rights; the constitutional rights, man, in behalf of myself; that's my constitutional right to talk in behalf of my constitutional rights.

COURT: Are you getting all of this, Miss Reporter?

REPORTER: Yes.

SEALE: I hope she gets it all. Taint the jury against me, send them threatening letters that I never sent and you know it's a lie; you keep them away from their homes and they blame me every time they come in this room because they are being kept away from their homes, and you did it.

COURT: Are you going to stop, sir?

SEALE: I am going to talk in behalf of my constitutional rights.

COURT: I note your counsel has remained quiet during your dissertation.

SEALE: You know what? I have no counsel here. I fired that lawyer before that jury heard anything and you know it. That jury hasn't heard all of the motions you denied behind the scenes. How you tricked that juror out of the stand by threatening her with that jive letter that you know damned well I didn't send, which is a lie, and they blame me every time they are being kept from their loved ones and their homes. They blame me every time they come in the room. I never sent those letters and you know it.

COURT: The Court will be in recess until tomorrow morning at ten o'clock.

CLERK: Will all please rise.

SEALE: I am not rising. I am not rising until he recognizes my constitutional rights. Why should I rise for him?

COURT: Mr. Marshal . . .

SEALE: I am not rising.

COURT: Mr. Marshal, see that he rises.

CLERK: Mr. Seale . . .

COURT: Get all of the defendants to rise.

CLERK: Mr. Hayden, will you please rise?

COURT: Let the record show that the defendant Mr. Hayden has not risen. I would request counsel to tell their clients—Mr. Kunstler, will you advise your clients to rise?

KUNSTLER: If the court please, it is my understanding that there is no constitutional or legal obligation on the part of a defendant to rise so long as his failure to rise is not disruptive.

COURT: You advise your clients not to rise, do you?

KUNSTLER: They are in protest of what you have done to Bobby Seale's right to defend himself.

COURT: Will you advise your clients to rise, Mr. Kunstler?

KUNSTLER: Your Honor, if you direct me to, I will advise them.

COURT: I direct you to.

KUNSTLER: Then I will pass on the direction, but I cannot in good conscience do more than that. They are free and independent, and they have to do what they please.

COURT: Let the record show that none of the defendants has risen.

Blackout.

SCENE FIVE
Testimony of Government Witness SERGEANT W. B. BAILEY
Chicago Police Officer

SCHULTZ: Would you relate what you heard, please?

BAILEY: I heard Mr. Rubin saying that "the pigs" started the violence, and he says, "Tonight we're not going to give up the park. We have to meet violence." He says, "The pigs are armed with guns and Mace, so we have to arm ourselves with"—any kind of weapon they could get.

SCHULTZ: Did he say anything more that you recall? Do you recall any further statements by him at this time?

BAILEY: I don't recall what else he said, but he ended up with saying, "And don't forget our gigantic love-in on the beaches tomorrow."

SCHULTZ: When the police car came, the marked police car came behind the barricade, did any of the people turn and face the police car?

BAILEY: Yes, they did.

SCHULTZ: Then what occurred, please?

BAILEY: Well, they began to throw rocks at it, boards, two-by-fours that were cut in half, hitting the car with it, breaking the windows. One took a piece of board that looked like an axe handle and started swinging at the blue light on the roof. The car went into the barricade and hit the barricade and then backed out and they were yelling, "Kill the pigs. Get them. Get those pigs in the car."

SCHULTZ: After the squad car left the area of the barricade, Sgt. Bailey, what occurred?

BAILEY: Shortly after, eight to ten patrolmen approached, spread out . . .

SCHULTZ: And what occurred please?

BAILEY: Objects came from the crowd, from behind the barricade again, bricks and stones mostly, bottles and cans, and one policeman turned, started running back, fell down, and they cheered and the policemen retreated.

SCHULTZ: What if anything did Mr. Rubin say during the preceding ten minutes before the policemen were assaulted which would encourage the crowd to assault the policemen?

BAILEY: He said, "Let's get the m-f-en pigs out of here." He said, "Take off your guns and we'll fight you," and "you're shitheads," and "you're m-f's," and "your kids are f-en pigs."

Blackout.

SCENE SIX
Testimony of Government Witness BARBARA BRADDOCK
Undercover Chicago Police Officer

SCHULTZ: Mrs. Braddock, who said, "Another good idea is golf balls"?

BRADDOCK: Abbie Hoffman said, "Another good idea is golf balls, with nails pounded through them in all different angles, so that when you throw them they will stick," and he said, "But don't forget the Vaseline for your faces to protect against the Mace, because there's going to be a lot of Mace flying, and don't forget your helmets, because you're going to need them to protect against the pigs." And then someone asked about holding the park that night, and he said, "Yeah, we should hold the park at all costs. It's our park, and the blank pigs have no right to push us out. It's our park and we're going to fight," and at that point my partner and I left.

SCHULTZ: Now, did you have occasion to see the defendant Rubin on Monday, August 26, 1968?

BRADDOCK: Yes, he was up on that table again with a megaphone making another speech.

SCHULTZ: Would you relate, please, what you recall of his speech?

BRADDOCK: He screamed into the megaphone, "The pigs aren't going to push us out of the park tonight! Let's get those bloodthirsty blankety-blank pigs!"

SCHULTZ: You say "blank pigs." Did he say "blank pigs"?

BRADDOCK: No, sir.

SCHULTZ: Did he use another word other than "blank"?

BRADDOCK: Yes, sir.

SCHULTZ: How many letters were in that word?

BRADDOCK: Four.

SCHULTZ: What was the first letter of the four-letter word, please?

BRADDOCK: "F."

RUBIN: What's the second letter, Barb?

SCHULTZ: That's all, Your Honor.

WEINGLASS: Your Honor, is that relevant? Are my clients being tried for that?

COURT: I don't ordinarily answer lawyer's questions, but since you asked so politely, I say yes.

WEINGLASS: It is relevant?

COURT: That is right. (*To* KUNSTLER.) Do you want to ask this witness some questions?

KUNSTLER: I might take a fling at it.

COURT: Oh, don't fling. Oh, no. We don't allow flings, but we will let you cross-examine the witness.

KUNSTLER: Thank you.

COURT: You're very welcome. Please proceed, Mr. Kunstler.

KUNSTLER: What drew your attention first to the man you say is Jerry Rubin, which is half an hour before he spoke as I understand it?

BRADDOCK: To be quite frank, I found him to be a very obnoxious man and . . .

RUBIN: Objection.

HOFFMAN: Sustained.

KUNSTLER: Go ahead. You have something else to say?

BRADDOCK: Yes, please. And this drew my attention to him and I just started to follow him.

KUNSTLER: Is your attention often drawn to obnoxious men?

SCHULTZ: Objection.

COURT: Sustained.

RUBIN: Bill, I do not follow people around in the parks for a living . . .

SCHULTZ: If the Court please, I ask that the defendant Rubin not speak aloud for everyone to hear. If the Court please.

KUNSTLER: Your Honor, he is speaking to me.

COURT: The defendant Rubin and others. I do direct them and the defendant Rubin not to speak aloud.

KUNSTLER: You said, I think, every other word was an obscenity?

BRADDOCK: Every other word was the "F" word.

KUNSTLER: What obscenity is that?

BRADDOCK: Pardon me? It is a four-letter word. Would you like me . . . I am not in the habit of saying it.

KUNSTLER: You have heard it, have you not?

BRADDOCK: Oh, yes.

KUNSTLER: You have heard it at the station house, haven't you?

FORAN: Your Honor, I object to that man . . .

KUNSTLER: I am not "that man," Mr. Foran. I have a name—William M. Kunstler.

FORAN: Do you really? Do you really?

KUNSTLER: And use my name. You use my name when you call me and not "that man."

FORAN: What I think of calling you I wouldn't say before ladies.

KUNSTLER: Your Honor . . .

COURT: I sustain Mr. Foran's objection. Mr. Kunstler, there is a great architect, Mr. Mies van der Rohe, who lately left us. He designed that witness box as well as this building, and it is a witness box, not a leaning post. I have asked you to stand behind it when you question the witness.

KUNSTLER: Your Honor, I think the U.S. Attorney questions from this witness box here . . .

COURT: I don't permit lawyers to lean on that thing. I don't want you to do it. I have asked you before. That was put there by the government, designed by Mr. van der Rohe, and I want you to use it for that purpose.

KUNSTLER: Your Honor, the U.S. Attorney questions from this witness box and leans on it.

COURT: I don't care about that.

KUNSTLER: Why am I different?

COURT: I haven't seen the United States Attorney lean on it as though it was a leaning post and I wouldn't permit them to do it or you.

KUNSTLER: Perhaps I am tired, Your Honor. What is wrong about leaning on it?

COURT: If you are tired, let Mr. . . .

KUNSTLER: Weinglass.

COURT: . . . Weinglass take over. Maybe I am tired, but I am sitting up here . . .

KUNSTLER: You are sitting in a comfortable chair.

COURT: I sit in the place where I should sit.

KUNSTLER: While I am standing up.

COURT: I will not permit you to lean on that. If you are tired we can take a recess and you can go to sleep for the afternoon.

KUNSTLER: I am not that tired, Your Honor.

COURT: Then please continue, Mr. Kunstler.

KUNSTLER: Thank you, Your Honor.

COURT: Yes, you're very welcome.

KUNSTLER: Can you describe what Mr. Hayden looked like then?

BRADDOCK: His hair was fairly close to regular length. I don't remember a moustache or anything. Sort of beady eyes.

KUNSTLER: Beady eyes?

BRADDOCK: Yes.

KUNSTLER: You don't like these defendants at all do you?

FORAN: Object to that.

COURT: Objection sustained.

KUNSTLER: Nothing further.

COURT: Is there any redirect?

SEALE: I would like to cross-examine the witness.

COURT: Mr. Seale . . .

SEALE: I want to cross-examine the witness.

COURT: Please be quiet, sir.

SEALE: My constitutional rights have been violated.

COURT: I order you to be quiet.

SEALE: I have a right to cross-examine the witness.

COURT: Now I want to tell you, Mr. Seale, again—you are not to intrude upon these proceedings in an improper manner.

SEALE: I have never intruded until it was the proper time for me to ask . . .

COURT: I must tell you sir, that if you are going to persist in this sort of thing, the Court will have to deal appropriately with your conduct.

Blackout.

SCENE SEVEN
Testimony of Government Witness ROBERT CONNELLY
Undercover Investigator

WEINGLASS: As things quieted down, did you see the police form a line?

CONNELLY: The line that I recall seeing had already formed, and it was partially into the crowd where the speakers on the microphone systems were telling the crowd to sit down, and then as the crowd sat down, the police retreated also.

WEINGLASS: Can you tell the jury in what manner the police came into the crowd? Was there a formation?

CONNELLY: Yes sir, there was.

WEINGLASS: Describe the formation of the police.

CONNELLY: It was a wedge-type formation.

WEINGLASS: How would you describe a wedge-type formation specifically?

CONNELLY: A "V" shape.

WEINGLASS: Were these policemen armed?

CONNELLY: Well, all uniformed police officers are armed.

WEINGLASS: What were they armed with?

CONNELLY: From what I could see they had their standard equipment.

WEINGLASS: Will you describe what they had in their hands as they went into that crowd?

CONNELLY: They had batons.

WEINGLASS: How were they holding their batons? Could you indicate that to the jury?

CONNELLY: When the wedge first started coming into the crowd, they were holding their batons, I believe, with both hands.

WEINGLASS: And did they begin to use their batons?

CONNELLY: Yes, sir, I believe they did.

WEINGLASS: With one hand?

CONNELLY: Yes, sir.

WEINGLASS: In a swinging fashion?

CONNELLY: Yes, sir.

WEINGLASS: Striking the people in front of them?

CONNELLY: Yes, sir.

WEINGLASS: Did you see anybody go down under the force and impact of the batons?

CONNELLY: Of the wedge coming in, yes, people were falling down and running back.

WEINGLASS: Did you see anyone get hit on the head with a baton?

CONNELLY: I don't recall seeing anyone go down as a result of being struck with a baton.

WEINGLASS: Did you see anyone get hit on the head with a baton?

CONNELLY: No, I couldn't say that.

WEINGLASS: Did you see anyone get hit on the head with a baton?

CONNELLY: I saw clubs swung at people's heads, yes.

WEINGLASS: By the police?

CONNELLY: Yes.

WEINGLASS: So, the police were swinging their clubs over their heads and down on the demonstrators?

CONNELLY: Yes, sir.

FORAN: Objection.

COURT: Sustained.

Blackout.

SCENE EIGHT
October 9, 1969

KUNSTLER: Your Honor, we have an emergency motion for a mistrial based on the following facts: Yesterday in the afternoon session, Stu Ball, who is the staff of the Defense, was called out of the court by a marshal who told Mr. Ball that there were two people outside who wanted to speak to him. When he arrived outside, he found four people. One of them told him he was under arrest; two informed him that they were agents of the Federal Bureau of Investigation. The two who indicated they were federal agents left the elevator going down and did not go to police headquarters at 11th and State. At police headquarters, Mr. Ball was taken to the police intelligence room, where he was forced to turn over a multitude of documents relating to the defense of this case. Mr. Ball informed them that he was a member of the legal defense staff of "the Conspiracy," and that the information in the documents was privileged, and that police intelligence officers have no right to see it. We feel, as did Mr. Ball, that they were shown by police intelligence officers to the federal officials conducting this trial, and who have had intimate relationships, as Your Honor knows from the people who have taken the stand here, with members of the Chicago Police Department—and particularly with members of the so-called "Red Squad." Mr. Ball asked them to return the documents, but they had been out of his sight for fifteen minutes, and it is our feeling that during that time they were photostated or Xeroxed by the Chicago Police Department. So I ask either for a mistrial or at least for a hearing by Your Honor of what we consider a flagrant breach of our own security, and a violation of the laws and Constitution of the United States.

COURT: The motion of the defendants for a mistrial will be denied.

Blackout.

SCENE NINE
Testimony of Government Witness WILLIAM ALBRIGHT
Undercover Operative

ALBRIGHT: Yes, I was with a fellow known as Gorilla who headed a motorcycle gang, and another fellow by the name of Banana. I was introduced to Abbie Hoffman as one of his bodyguards.

KUNSTLER: Yes, and yesterday you testified that you had been or were a student at Northwestern Illinois State College?

ALBRIGHT: That is right, sir.

KUNSTLER: You were expelled, were you not, for throwing the president off the stage physically?

ALBRIGHT: No, I was not, sir.

KUNSTLER: What were you expelled for?

ALBRIGHT: I was expelled for being with a group of people that threw the president off the stage.

WEINGLASS: Mr. Albright, you testified yesterday and, I believe, on Friday, that you were functioning in an undercover capacity for the Police Department of the City of Chicago on August 17, 1968, when you were at a meeting in Grant Park, and I believe you testified that it was you who suggested to the meeting the method and the manner in which public lavatories could be sabotaged, is that correct?

ALBRIGHT: No, sir.

WEINGLASS: Then correct me on that. What did you tell the group?

ALBRIGHT: I related a story.

WEINGLASS: In relating that story, did you tell the group that another group of people placed balsawood balls in the lavatory and that caused the lavatory not to function?

ALBRIGHT: Yes, that was part of the story.

WEINGLASS: Was it part of your instruction or part of your police assignment to tell demonstrators in this city funny stories about how they could sabotage public lavatories?

ALBRIGHT: I don't recall, sir.

WEINGLASS: At this meeting it was you who suggested that grappling hooks and ropes be used to stop jeeps that had barbed wire on the front of them, is that correct?

ALBRIGHT: That is not correct, sir.

WEINGLASS: Tell us what you suggested to Rennie Davis.

ALBRIGHT: I suggested to Rennie Davis and some other people that a grappling hook be thrown into the barbed wire as it was being strung out from a truck.

WEINGLASS: From a truck?

ALBRIGHT: Yes, sir.

WEINGLASS: Is that from a military truck?

ALBRIGHT: I don't know, sir.

WEINGLASS: What kind of truck did you have in mind when you said it?

ALBRIGHT: Truck.

WEINGLASS: Any kind of truck? A moving van?

ALBRIGHT: Do you want an exact description of the truck, sir?

WEINGLASS: Yes, if you can, give us the exact description of it, if you have it.

ALBRIGHT: Something like a two-and-a-half-ton military truck, with a canopy on the back of it.

WEINGLASS: You suggested that a grappling hook be used to somehow interfere with the wire mechanism of that truck? Is that correct?

ALBRIGHT: Yes, I did, sir.

WEINGLASS: People were asking for suggestions, but you were the only one to suggest that a military vehicle should be sabotaged, isn't that true?

ALBRIGHT: I think there were other suggestions, sir!

WEINGLASS: Now, I call your attention to Tuesday night, August 27th. You testified you attended a meeting in Grant Park. Is that correct?

ALBRIGHT: Yes, sir.

WEINGLASS: Was this one of the nights you were throwing rocks at the police yourself?

ALBRIGHT: I don't recall having thrown a rock on Tuesday night at the police.

WEINGLASS: Is it possible you might have thrown a can or stick, or some other object to provoke the police?

ALBRIGHT: I might have thrown a can of paint later on that evening.

WEINGLASS: Do you recall being asked by the grand jury the following question: "Mr. Albright, do you recall having seen Jerry Rubin throwing an object at the police?"

SCHULTZ: If the Court please, what he should ask him: "Did you see Jerry Rubin throw an object at the police?" If he says "yes," then he can read this question and answer.

COURT: It seems to me, Mr., er, Weinglass, those are two different situations.

WEINGLASS: If Your Honor please, I've spent a good deal of time with this witness . . .

COURT: I have spent a good deal of time listening to you, also. Do you want a gold star for the time you spent?

KUNSTLER: Your Honor, I object to that, those insulting remarks, to cocounsel.

COURT: I don't insult lawyers.

KUNSTLER: Sir, you just have, Your Honor.

COURT: Don't make a suggestion like that again, sir. If you will sit down, Mr. . . . .

KUNSTLER: Kunstler is the name, K-U-N-S-T-L-E-R.

COURT: I will let my ruling stand. Please continue Mr. . . . .

WEINGLASS: Weinglass, Your Honor. Did you, yourself, ever recall having seen Jerry Rubin throw an object at the police? Jerry Rubin?

ALBRIGHT: At the police themselves, *no.*

WEINGLASS: Thank you very much.

COURT: Is there any redirect examination?

SCHULTZ: Yes, Your Honor.

SEALE: Before the redirect, I would like to request again—demand—that I be able to cross-examine this witness. My lawyer is not here; I think I have a right to defend myself in this courtroom.

COURT: Let the record show the defendant Seale is again speaking in direct contempt of court.

SEALE: I would like to request that I be able to cross-examine the witness.

COURT: I deny your request, Mr. Seale.

SEALE: What about Section 1982, Title 42 of the code where it says the black man cannot be discriminated against in any legal defense in any court in America?

COURT: Mr. Seale, do not attempt to indoctrinate me as to what the law says.

SEALE: You have George Washington and Thomas Jefferson standing in pictures behind you, and they were slave owners. That's what they were. They owned slaves. You are acting in the same manner, denying me my constitutional rights of being able to cross-examine this witness. You have heard direct examination, we have cross-examination by the other defendants' lawyers, and I have a right to cross-examine the witness.

COURT: Mr. Seale, I have admonished you previously . . .

SEALE: I have a right to cross-examine this witness.

COURT: . . . what might happen to you if you keep on talking. Mr. Kunstler has his appearance on record here as your attorney.

SEALE: He is not. He is not. He is not my lawyer and you know that.

COURT: He is. I don't know . . .

SEALE: You know that.

COURT: I know that he is, and I know that this is an entire device here . . .

SEALE: He is not my lawyer; you have forced—you have made your choice of who you think should represent me. That is not true. I made the choice of Charles R. Garry to represent me.

COURT: We are going to recess now, young man. If you keep this . . .

SEALE: Look, old man, if you keep denying me my constitutional rights . . .

SCHULTZ: May the record show, if the Court please, that while the marshals were restraining Bobby Seale, the defendant Dellinger physically attempted to interfere.

COURT: I am warning you, sir, that the law . . .

SEALE: Instead of warning, why don't you warn me that I have got a right to defend myself, huh?

COURT: I am warning you that the Court has a right to gag you. I don't want to do that. Under the law you may be gagged and chained to your chair.

SEALE: Gagged? I am being railroaded already.

COURT: And I might add, since it has been said here that all the defendants support you in your position, that I might conclude that they are bad risks for bail, and I say that to you, Mr. Kunstler, that if you can't control your client . . .

SEALE: I demand my right to be able to cross-examine this witness. He has made statements against me and I want my right to defend myself in this trial. I want my rights recognized.

COURT: Mr. Kunstler, I will address you if you stand up.

KUNSTLER: I was going to address you, Your Honor, because you made some remarks . . .

SEALE: He doesn't represent me. You can address him all you want. He doesn't represent me. He doesn't represent me.

KUNSTLER: Your Honor, they said this morning they fully supported his right to defend himself or have a lawyer of his choice, and if that is the price of their bail, then I guess that will have to be the price of their bail.

COURT: Let me tell you . . .

SEALE: I have the right to defend myself. That's what you . . .

COURT: Will Mr. Marshal have that man sit down.

MARSHAL: Mr. Seale, sit down.

SEALE: You are trying to make jive bargaining operations and that's different from the right I have. I have a right to speak out on behalf of my defense and you know it. You know it. Why don't you recognize my right to defend myself?

COURT: Mr. Seale . . .

SEALE: I request again—demand, to cross-examine the witness.

COURT: I will issue the orders around here.

SEALE: I don't take orders from racist judges. We protested our rights for 400 years and we have been shot and killed and murdered, brutalized and oppressed for 400 years.

COURT: Did you get that outburst, Miss Reporter?

REPORTER: Yes, sir.

COURT: If you continue with that sort of thing, you may expect to be punished. I warned you right through this trial and I warn you again, sir.

SEALE: Why don't you knock me on the mouth? Try that. You represent the corruptness of this rotten, fascist government for 400 years.

COURT: I will tell you what I indicated yesterday might happen to you . . .

SEALE: Happen to me? What can happen to me more than what Thomas Jefferson and George Washington did to black people in slavery?

COURT: Have him sit down, Mr. Marshal. Well, I have been called a racist, a fascist. He has pointed to the picture of George Washington and called him a slave owner and . . .

SEALE: They were slave owners. Look at history.

COURT: As though I had anything to do with that.

KUNSTLER: We all share a common guilt, Your Honor.

SEALE: You have done everything you could with those jive lying witnesses up there presented by these pig agents of the Government to lie and condone some rotten fascist, racist crap by racist cops and pigs that beat people's heads . . .

COURT: Mr. Seale, do you want to stop or do you want me to direct the Marshal . . .

SEALE: . . . and I demand my constitutional rights—demand, demand, demand!

COURT: Take the defendant into the room and deal with him as he should be dealt with in this circumstance! We will take a recess!

Blackout.

"The proper course for the trial judge was to have restrained the defendant by whatever means necessary, even if those means include his being shackled and gagged."

—Appeals Court Decision

U.S. ex rei *Allen v. State of Illinois,* June, 1969

SCENE TEN

(Seale is brought in, bound to a chair.)

FORAN: Your Honor, if Mr. Seale would express to the Court his willingness to be quiet, would the Court entertain the possibility of Mr. Seale being unbound and un-gagged?

COURT: I have tried with all my heart to get him to sit in this Court and be tried fairly, and I have been greeted on every occasion with all sorts of vicious invective. Mr. Seale, all of your Constitutional and statutory rights have been and will be preserved in this trial. I want you to conduct yourself in a manner that is gentlemanly. I ask you, therefore, and you may indicate by raising your head up and down, or shaking your head side to side, meaning no, whether or not I have your assurance that you will not disrupt this trial if you are permitted to resume your former place. Will you, sir?

SEALE: *(Gagged.)* I can't speak.

COURT: I can't understand you.

SEALE: *(Gagged.)* I want to defend myself.

COURT: Mr. Marshal. *(Gag tightened.)* Well, Mr. Foran, I tried to do what you suggested.

FORAN: Your Honor. I would also like the record to show that just prior to Mr. Seale speaking through his gag, the defendant Davis was whispering to him. Encouraging him.

COURT: Mr. Seale, I order you to refrain from making those noises.

Now, Mr. Foran, do you have any redirect examination of this witness?

KUNSTLER: Your Honor, before Mr. Foran proceeds, I just want to move for the removal of the irons and the gag on the ground that Mr. Seale was attempting to assert his right of self-defense under the Constitution.

COURT: These measures have been taken to ensure the proper conduct of this trial, which I am obligated to do under the law. The motion of Mr. Kunstler will be denied.

Blackout.

SCENE ELEVEN
Testimony of Government Witness RICHARD GRANDHOLM
Chicago Police Officer

COURT: Will you continue with your cross-examination?

WEINGLASS: If Your Honor please, just before that I would like to inform the Court that, standing here as I am just five feet from a man who is shackled and bound and gagged, and who, when the jury is not in this courtroom . . .

COURT: Will you continue with your cross-examination?

WEINGLASS: . . . is physically assaulted by the marshals . . .

COURT: If you have any observation about any other thing, I will permit you to make it at the end of your cross-examination.

WEINGLASS: I am attempting to . . .

COURT: Please continue with your cross-examination of this witness.

WEINGLASS: After you heard Mr. Froines make that speech, did you make any arrests?

GRANDHOLM: No, sir.

WEINGLASS: Now, you did see what you described as a couple making love in a tree, did you not?

GRANDHOLM: I did.

WEINGLASS: You saw them having intercourse in a tree, isn't that correct?

GRANDHOLM: Yes, sir.

WEINGLASS: And that was what kind of tree, do you remember?

GRANDHOLM: I don't know what kind of tree it was, sir.

WEINGLASS: You're quite sure you hadn't wandered into the zoo.

GRANDHOLM: Quite sure.

WEINGLASS: Did you arrest those people?

GRANDHOLM: No, sir.

WEINGLASS: In fact you went right under the tree and you looked up, isn't that correct?

GRANDHOLM: No, sir, I was under . . .

WEINGLASS: You weren't under the tree looking up?

GRANDHOLM: I was under the tree. I didn't walk under. I was under there at the time.

WEINGLASS: And then suddenly your attention was drawn to the fact that someone was making love over your head, isn't that correct?

GRANDHOLM: That is right.

WEINGLASS: And you looked up?

GRANDHOLM: I did.

WEINGLASS: How long did you look?

GRANDHOLM: Two seconds.

WEINGLASS: And then you walked on about your business, is that correct?

GRANDHOLM: Yes, sir.

WEINGLASS: Were you concerned about their safety?

GRANDHOLM: No, sir.

KUNSTLER: If Your Honor please, the cuff holding Mr. Seale's hand is digging into his hand, and he appears to be trying to free his hand from that pressure. Could he be assisted?

COURT: If the marshal has concluded that he needs assistance, of course.

MARSHAL: No, Your Honor.

COURT: Please continue with your cross-examination, Mr. Weinstein.

WEINGLASS: Weinglass, Your Honor. If Your Honor please, Mr. Seale is having difficulty. He is in extreme discomfort.

COURT: He is being treated in accordance with the law.

KUNSTLER: Not the Constitution of the United States, Your Honor, which is the supreme law. He has the right to defend himself.

COURT: I don't need someone to come here from New York or wherever it is you come from to tell me that there is a Constitution in the United States.

KUNSTLER: I feel someone needs to tell someone, Your Honor. It is not being observed in this Court, if that is the treatment a man gets for defending himself.

COURT: Read the books. You read the books and you will find that the

Court has the authority to do what is being done, and I will not let this trial be broken up by his conduct.

KUNSTLER: Your Honor, we feel that it is impossible for white men to sit in this room while a black man is in chains and continue . . .

COURT: I wish you wouldn't talk about the distinction between white and black in this courtroom.

KUNSTLER: A lot of the seven white men . . .

COURT: I have lived a long time and you are the first person who has ever suggested that I have discriminated against a black man. Come into my chambers and I will show you on the wall what one of the great newspapers of this city said about me in respect to the school segregation case.

KUNSTLER: Your Honor, this is not a time for self-praise on either side of the bench.

COURT: It isn't self-praise, sir. It is defense. I won't have a lawyer stand before the bar and accuse me of being a bigot.

KUNSTLER: For God's sakes, Your Honor, we are seeking a solution of a human problem here, not whether you feel good or bad.

COURT: Don't shout at me. I don't like that. (*To* WEINGLASS.) Mr. . . . .

WEINGLASS: It is impossible for me at this point to proceed with the cross-examination of this witness, while one man is here receiving the treatment that Mr. Seale is being dealt at your hand.

COURT: If it isn't possible, then you may sit down. Do you want to continue with your examination?

WEINGLASS: I do not.

COURT: Then you may sit down.

SCHULTZ: Your Honor, I think we are, of course, concerned. He looks very uncomfortable.

KUNSTLER: Your Honor, are we going to stop this medieval torture that is going on in this courtroom? I think this is a disgrace.

SEALE: The motherfucker is tight and it is stopping my blood.

COURT: Listen to him now.

KUNSTLER: Your Honor, we cannot hear him because of the binding and gag on him.

COURT: Why should I have to go through a trial and be assailed in an obscene manner?

DAVIS: Ladies and gentlemen of the jury, he was being tortured while you were out of this room, by these marshals. It is terrible what is happening.

COURT: Will you ask that man to sit down, Mr. Marshal?

FORAN: That is Mr. Davis, Your Honor.

HAYDEN: Your Honor, could I address you?

COURT: No, you may not, sir. You have a lawyer; that is what lawyers are for.

HAYDEN: All I want to say is that . . .

COURT: Sit down, please.

HAYDEN: Bobby Seale should not be put in a position of slavery.

COURT: Mr. Marshal, tell that man to sit down. What is his name?

HAYDEN: My name is Tom Hayden, Your Honor. I would just like to . . .

COURT: Let the record show that Mr. Tom Hayden persisted in speaking despite the Court's direction that he sit down. Who is that man who is talking?

FROINES: Your Honor, he is being choked to death, tortured . . .

SEALE: The judge is not—he is not trying to give you no fair trial.

COURT: Mr. Marshal . . . (*The* MARSHALS *remove* SEALE.)

HOFFMAN: You may as well kill him if you are going to gag him.

FORAN: That was the defendant Hoffman who spoke.

COURT: You are not permitted to address the Court, Mr. Hoffman. You have a lawyer.

HOFFMAN: This isn't a court. This is an inquisition!

KUNSTLER: Can we have somebody with Mr. Seale? We don't trust those marshals.

COURT: The marshals will take care of him.

RUBIN: Take care of him?

HAYDEN: Yeah, they're taking care of him right now by beating him!

COURT: Let that appear on the record, Miss Reporter.

Blackout.

"We don't hate white people, we hate the oppressor: if the oppressor is white, then we hate him."
—Huey Newton, Minister of Defense,
Black Panther Party

SCENE TWELVE
November 3, 1969
(Seale is brought in handcuffed and gagged.)

COURT: I find that the acts, statements, and conduct of the defendant Bobby Seale constitute a deliberate and willful attack upon the administration of justice, and attempt to sabotage the functioning of the federal judiciary system and misconduct of so grave a character as to make the mere imposition of a fine a futile gesture, and a wholly insignificant punishment. Accordingly, I adjudge Bobby G. Seale guilty of each and every contempt specification referred to in my oral observations of direct contempt of Court. The defendant Seale will be committed to the custody of the Attorney General of the United States for imprisonment for a term of three months on each and every specification, the sentences to run consecutively. (*To* DEFENDANTS.) Quiet! Mr. Seale, you have the right to speak now. I will hear you. (*The gag is removed.*)

SEALE: For myself?

COURT: In your own behalf, yes.

SEALE: How come I couldn't speak before?

COURT: This is a special occasion.

SEALE: Wait a minute. Now are you going to try—you punish me for attempting to speak for myself before? Now after you punish me, you sit up there and say something about "you can speak"? What kind of jive is that? I don't understand it. What kind of court is this? Is this a court? It must be some kind of fascist operation like I see in my mind, you know—I don't understand you.

COURT: I am calling on you . . .

SEALE: What am I supposed to speak about? I still haven't got the right to defend myself. I would like to speak about that. I would like to—since you let me stand up and speak, can I speak about—can I defend myself?

COURT: I have tried to make it clear.

SEALE: All you can make clear to me is that you don't want me. You don't want to listen to me. If a black man stands up and speaks, if a black man demands his rights, if a black requests and argues his rights, what do you do? You're talking about punishing.

COURT: I direct the United States Attorney to prepare from the oral remarks I made here a certificate of contempt for my signature, together with a judgment and commitment order. How soon, Miss Reporter, before it is written? I am glad I have got both of you here.

REPORTER: Six o'clock, Your Honor.

COURT: Get it to Mr. Foran as soon as you can, and the case will be continued until tomorrow morning. There will be an order declaring a mistrial as to the defendant Bobby G. Seale, and not as to any other defendants.

SEALE: What's the cat trying to pull now? I'm leaving the—I can't stay?

SCHULTZ: Will Your Honor set a trial date for the defendant Seale?

COURT: Yes. Yes.

SEALE: I demand an immediate trial right now.

COURT: Yes, we will give you a trial date.

SEALE: I'm talking about now. I don't want to be taken out. I have a right to go through with this trial.

COURT: A mistrial has been declared with respect to you, sir. Your trial will be conducted on April 23, 1970, at ten o'clock in the morning.

SEALE: I want it immediate, right now, though.

COURT: I'm sorry, I can't try two cases at one time, sir.

SEALE: I still want an immediate trial. You can't call it a mistrial. I'm put in jail for four months for nothing? I want . . .

COURT: All right, Mr. Marshal . . .

KUNSTLER: Your Honor . . .

SEALE: I want . . .

COURT: Mr. Marshal.

KUNSTLER: The right of a black man to defend himself . . .

COURT: I will not hear you any longer.

FORAN: No man, black, white, green, or polka-dotted has any right to disrupt a Court of the United States.

SEALE: I'm not disrupting . . .

HAYDEN: Now they are going to beat him!

DELLINGER: Somebody go to protect him!

FORAN: Your Honor, may the record show that that is Mr. Dellinger saying "someone go to protect him" . . .

RUBIN: May the record show that Foran is a Nazi.

FORAN: And the other comment is by Mr. Rubin.

SCHULTZ: And after that it was Mr. Hayden, Your Honor.

HAYDEN: I was trying to protect Mr. Seale, Your Honor. A man is supposed to be quiet when he sees another's nose being smashed?!

KUNSTLER: This is not a court, Your Honor. It's a medieval torture chamber.

FORAN: That man goes on and on.

COURT: Everything you say will be taken down.

SEALE: You fascist dogs.

KUNSTLER: Your Honor, this is a disgrace. We would like the names of these marshals . . .

COURT: Don't point at me in that manner.

KUNSTLER: Your Honor, this is an unholy disgrace to the law.

FORAN: Created by Mr. Kunstler.

KUNSTLER: Created by nothing other than what you have done to this man.

SEALE: You low-life son of a bitch. (MARSHAL *strikes* SEALE. RUBIN *leaps over the defense table.*)

COURT: Did you get that Miss Reporter?

KUNSTLER: They are assaulting the other defendants, as well!

HOFFMAN: You come down here and watch it, Judge. It's the same thing that happened last year in Chicago, the exact same thing!

COURT: Take that down. The Court will be in recess!

Blackout.

Bobby Seale with Chicago Black Panther leader Fred Hampton and others at defense attorneys' offices during pretrial meetings, spring 1969. NACIO JAN BROWN

ACT TWO

No. 69 Crim. -180 United States of America, Plaintiff

David T. Dellinger, Rennard C. Davis, Thomas E. Hayden, Abbott H. Hoffman, Jerry C. Rubin, Lee Weiner and John R. Froines, Defendants

SCENE ONE
Case for the Defense
Vietnam Moratorium Day
October 15, 1969

CLERK: Will all please rise. (JUDGE *enters.*) United States District Court for the Northern District of Illinois is now in session. The Honorable Julius J. Hoffman presiding. Please be seated.

(*The names of war dead are read by the* DEFENDANTS.)

DELLINGER: Mr. Hoffman, we are observing the Vietnam Moratorium.

COURT: I am Judge Hoffman, sir.

DELLINGER: I believe in equality, sir, so I prefer to call people Mr. or by their first name.

COURT: Sit down. The clerk is about to call the case.

DELLINGER: I want to explain to you, we are reading the names of the war dead.

MARSHAL: Sit down, Mr. Dellinger. (*The* MARSHALS *confiscate the lists.*)

DELLINGER: We were reading the names of the dead from both sides.

MARSHAL: Sit down.

DELLINGER: All right. I'll sit down.

CLERK: No. 69CR 180. United States of America v. David T. Dellinger, et al. Case on trial.

KUNSTLER: Your Honor, the defendants, who were not permitted to be absent today or to have a court recess for the Vietnam Moratorium, brought in an American flag and a National Liberation Front flag which they placed on the counsel table to commemorate the dead Americans and the dead Vietnamese in this long and brutal war.

COURT: We have an American flag in the corner. Haven't you seen it during the three and a half months you have been here?

KUNSTLER: Yes, but we wanted the juxtaposition of the two flags together in one place.

COURT: I point out, standing in the courtroom—and it has been here since this building was opened—is an American flag.

HOFFMAN: We don't consider this table a part of the courtroom and we want to furnish it in our own way.

MARSHAL: Sit down.

COURT: To place the flag of an enemy country . . .

KUNSTLER: No, Your Honor. There is no declared war.

HAYDEN: Are you at war with Vietnam?

COURT: Any country—let that appear on the record. I will ask you to sit down.

KUNSTLER: Your Honor . . .

FORAN: Your Honor, this is outrageous. This man is a mouthpiece. Look at him, wearing an armband like his clients.

COURT: Note has been duly made on the record.

KUNSTLER: Your Honor, I just want to object to Mr. Foran yelling in the presence of the jury . . .

FORAN: Oh, Your Honor . . .

KUNSTLER: Your Honor, I think that the expression on Mr. Foran's face speaks louder than any picture can tell . . .

FORAN: Of my contempt for Mr. Kunstler, Your Honor.

KUNSTLER: I am wearing an armband in memoriam to the dead, Your Honor, which is no disgrace in this country. I want him admonished, Your Honor.

COURT: Did you say you want to admonish me?

KUNSTLER: No. I want you to admonish him.

COURT: Let the record show I do not admonish the United States Attorney because he was properly representing his client, the United States of America.

DELLINGER: We would like to propose . . .

SCHULTZ: If the Court please . . .

FORAN: If the Court please, Your Honor, may the marshal take that man into custody.

DELLINGER: A moment of silence . . .

SCHULTZ: Your Honor, this man . . .

DELLINGER: We only want a moment of silence . . .

SCHULTZ: Your Honor, this man said on the elevator on the way up here . . .

DELLINGER: We only want a moment of silence.

FORAN: Your Honor, I object to this man speaking out in court.

COURT: You needn't object. I forbid him to disrupt the Court. I note for the record that his name is . . .

DELLINGER: David Dellinger is my name.

COURT: You needn't interrupt my sentence for me.

DELLINGER: You have been interrupting ours.

COURT: The name of this man who has attempted to disrupt the proceedings is David Dellinger, and the record will clearly indicate that, Miss Reporter.

Blackout.

Rennie Davis at defense attorneys' offices during pretrial meetings, spring 1969.
NACIO JAN BROWN

SCENE TWO
Testimony of Defendant RENNARD C. DAVIS

FORAN: Objection.

COURT: Sustained.

WEINGLASS: Could you relate now to the Court and jury the words you spoke, as best as you can recall, on that particular night?

DAVIS: I began by holding up a small steel ball about the size of a tennis ball and I said, "This bomb was dropped on a city of 100,000 people, a city called Nam Ding, by an American fighter jet; about 640 of these steel balls were spewed into the sky from one large bomb." And I said, "When this ball strikes a building or the ground, an explosion occurs which sends out about 300 steel pellets. With 640 of these bombs going off, you can throw steel pellets over an area about a thousand yards long and about 250 yards wide, and every living thing exposed in that thousand-yard area will die." I said, "This bomb would not destroy this building, it would not damage the walls, the ceiling, the floor." I said, "If it is dropped on a city, it takes life but leaves the institutions. It is the ideal weapon, you see, for the mentality who reasons that life is less precious than property." I said that, in 1967, one out of every two bombs dropped on North Vietnam by the American government was this weapon. And in 1967 the American government told the American public that in North Vietnam it was hitting only military targets. Yet what I saw were pagodas that had been gutted, schoolhouses that had been razed, population centers that had been leveled.

WEINGLASS: If the Court please, the Defense would like to offer into evidence D-235, the anti-personnel bomb . . .

FORAN: Your Honor, the Government objects to this exhibit. The Vietnamese war has nothing whatsoever to do with the charges in this indictment.

COURT: I sustain the objection of the Government. Mr. Marshal, will you remove that man sitting there. Ask him to leave. He was laughing right at me while I was speaking.

WEINGLASS: I was standing right here. Mr. Ball did not laugh.

COURT: Mr. Ball was laughing right at me.

HAYDEN: Your Honor . . .

COURT: I ask Mr. Ball to leave.

HOFFMAN: I was laughing.

HAYDEN: It was me that was laughing, Your Honor.

COURT: I can't order you to leave. You are at trial. Mr. Marshal, take Mr. Ball out.

DELLINGER: This is an injustice.

KUNSTLER: That is a lawyer who is part of our defense team.

COURT: He is not a lawyer permitted to practice in this Court.

KUNSTLER: You are removing a lawyer from the defense table.

COURT: No, he is not a lawyer permitted to practice here.

KUNSTLER: That doesn't matter, Your Honor, he is . . .

DELLINGER: He wasn't laughing.

KUNSTLER: You have given him permission to sit here.

COURT: I withdraw the permission.

KUNSTLER: You are depriving us of a lawyer at our defense table.

COURT: That is just too bad. You will have to suffer through without him.

KUNSTLER: He is a member of the bar of the District of Columbia. He had been assisting us for three months through this trial.

COURT: Let him go back to the District of Columbia. I will not have him here while I am trying to rule.

KUNSTLER: But he didn't laugh, Your Honor. If he laughed that is one thing, perhaps, but two defendants have admitted laughing.

COURT: No, Mr. Ball will not be readmitted. He is not permitted to practice here, and for good and sufficient reason I order him out.

KUNSTLER: Put him in the stand and ask him whether he laughed.

COURT: Will you sit down, please.

KUNSTLER: He wouldn't lie under oath.

COURT: Will you sit down!

KUNSTLER: I guess I have no alternative, Your Honor.

COURT: That is right.

Blackout.

Abbie Hoffman in Chicago police uniform, spring 1969. NACIO JAN BROWN

SCENE THREE
Testimony of Defendant ABBOTT H. HOFFMAN

WEINGLASS: Will you please identify yourself for the record?

HOFFMAN: My name is Abbie. I am an orphan of America.

WEINGLASS: Where do you reside?

HOFFMAN: I live in Woodstock Nation.

WEINGLASS: Will you tell the Court and jury where that is?

HOFFMAN: Yes. It is a nation of alienated young people. We carry it around with us in the same way the Sioux Indians carried the Sioux Nation around with them. It is a nation dedicated to cooperation versus competition, to the idea that people should have a better means of exchange than property or money, that there should be some other basis for human interaction. It is a nation dedicated to . . .

COURT: Excuse me, sir. Read the question to the witness, please.

REPORTER: "Will you tell the Court and jury where it is?"

COURT: Just where it is, that's all.

HOFFMAN: It is in my mind and in the minds of my brothers and sisters. It does not consist of property or material, but rather of ideas and certain values, those values being cooperation versus competition, and . . .

SCHULTZ: That doesn't say where Woodstock Nation, whatever that is, is.

WEINGLASS: Your Honor, the witness has identified it as being a state of mind, and he has, I think, a right to define that state of mind.

HOFFMAN: This is going to be a very exciting cross-examination.

COURT: No, we want the place of residence, if he has one, place of doing business, if you have a business, or both, if you desire to tell both. One address will be sufficient. But nothing about philosophy or India, sir. Just where you live if you have a place to live. Now you said Woodstock. In what state is Woodstock?

HOFFMAN: It is the state of mind, in the mind of myself and my brothers and sisters. It's a conspiracy.

WEINGLASS: Abbie, could you tell the Court and jury . . .

SCHULTZ: His name isn't Abbie. I object to this informality.

COURT: Objection sustained. Yes, use his full name, Mr. Winegrass.

HOFFMAN: Winegrass, it's my favorite combination!

WEINGLASS: Can you tell the Court and jury your present age?

HOFFMAN: My age is 33. I am a child of the '60s.

WEINGLASS: When were you born?

HOFFMAN: Psychologically, 1960.

SCHULTZ: Objection.

COURT: I sustain the objection.

WEINGLASS: Between the date of your birth and May 1, 1960, what, if anything, occurred in your life?

HOFFMAN: Nothing. I believe it's called an American education.

SCHULTZ: Objection.

COURT: I sustain the objection.

HOFFMAN: Huh?

WEINGLASS: Can you tell the Court and jury what is your present occupation?

HOFFMAN: I am a cultural revolutionary. Well, I am really a defendant—full time.

WEINGLASS: Abbie Hoffman, prior to coming to Chicago, did you enter into an agreement with David Dellinger, John Froines, Tom Hayden, Jerry Rubin, Lee Weiner, or Rennie Davis, to come to the city of Chicago for the purpose of encouraging and promoting violence during the convention week?

HOFFMAN: An agreement?

WEINGLASS: Yes.

HOFFMAN: We couldn't agree on lunch.

SCHULTZ: It was in December of 1967 that you and Rubin and Paul Krassner created the Yippie myth, is that right?

HOFFMAN: And Nancy Kurshan and Anita Hoffman—that's the woman I live with. It's not just men that participate in myths.

SCHULTZ: And the myth was created in order to get people to come to Chicago, isn't that right, Mr. Hoffman?

HOFFMAN: That's right, Mr. Schultz—that was one reason, to create—the other was to put forth a certain concept, a certain lifestyle.

SCHULTZ: And part of your myth was "We'll burn Chicago to the ground," isn't that right?

HOFFMAN: It was part of the myth that there were trainloads of dynamite headed for Chicago; it was part of the myth that they were going to form white vigilante groups and round up demonstrators. All these things were part of the myth. A myth is a process of telling stories, most of which aren't true.

SCHULTZ: On the 7th of August, you told David Stahl you were going to have nude-ins in the parks of Chicago, didn't you?

HOFFMAN: A nude-in? I don't believe I would use that phrase, no. Quite frankly, I don't think it's very poetic.

SCHULTZ: You told him, did you not, Mr. Hoffman, that you would have . . .

HOFFMAN: I'm not even sure I know what it is, a nude-in.

SCHULTZ: Public fornication.

KUNSTLER: I object to this because Mr. Schultz is acting like a dirty old man.

SCHULTZ: No, we aren't getting into dirty old men here.

COURT: Objection denied.

HOFFMAN: I don't mind talking about it.

SCHULTZ: Mr. Hoffman—Your Honor, Mr. Davis is having a very fine time here whispering at me. He has been doing it for the last twenty minutes. I would ask Mr. Davis to stop distracting me.

COURT: Try not to speak too loudly, Mr. Davis.

DAVIS: Yes, sir.

COURT: Go ahead.

HOFFMAN: Go ahead, Dick.

SCHULTZ: "And there will be acid for all," that was another one of your Yippie myths, isn't that right?

HOFFMAN: That was well known.

SCHULTZ: Was there any acid in Lincoln Park in Chicago?

HOFFMAN: In the reservoir, in the lake?

SCHULTZ: No, among the people.

HOFFMAN: Among the people was there LSD? Well, there might have been. I don't know. It's colorless, odorless, and tasteless. One can never tell.

SCHULTZ: What about the honey? Was there anything special about any honey in Lincoln Park?

HOFFMAN: There was honey, there was—I was told there was honey—I was getting stoned eating brownies. Honey, yes. Lots of people were . . .

SCHULTZ: Was there LSD to your knowledge in both the honey and in some brownies? Is that right?

HOFFMAN: I would have to be a chemist to know that for a fact. It is colorless, odorless, and tasteless.

SCHULTZ: Didn't you state on a prior occasion that Ed Sanders passed out from too much honey?

HOFFMAN: Yes. People passed out.

COURT: You have answered the question.

HOFFMAN: Yes. Passed out from honey? Sure. Is that illegal?

SCHULTZ: And a man named Spade passed out on honey.

HOFFMAN: Yes. I made up that name. Frankie Spade, wasn't it? It must have been strong honey.

COURT: The last observation of the witness may go out and the witness is directed again not to make any gratuitous observations.

HOFFMAN: Where do they go when they go out?

COURT: Will you remain quiet while I am making a ruling? I know you have no respect for me.

KUNSTLER: Your Honor, that is totally unwarranted.

COURT: I don't need any argument on that one. The witness turned his back on me while he was on the witness stand.

HOFFMAN: I was just looking at the pictures of the longhairs up on the wall.

COURT: And I don't like being laughed at by a witness in this Court, sir.

HOFFMAN: I know that laughing is a crime. I already . . .

COURT: I direct you not to laugh at an observation by the Court. I don't laugh at you.

HOFFMAN: Are you sure?

COURT: I haven't laughed at you during all of the many weeks and months of this trial. Mr. Schultz, ask your next question, please.

SCHULTZ: Mr. Hoffman, isn't it a fact that one of the reasons why you came to Chicago was simply to wreck American society?

HOFFMAN: My feeling at the time, and still is, that this society is going to wreck itself. Our role is to survive. Could I have a glass of water, Judge?

COURT: Give him some water, please.

HOFFMAN: This trial is bad for my health.

WEINGLASS: Now, in exorcising the Pentagon, were there any plans to raise the building off the ground?

HOFFMAN: Yes. When we were arrested they asked us what we were doing. We said it was to measure the Pentagon and we wanted a permit to raise it 300 feet in the air, and they said, "How about ten?" So we said, "Okay." And they threw us out of the Pentagon and we went back to New York and had a press conference and told them what it was about. We also introduced a drug called "lace," which, when you squirted it at policemen it made them take their clothes off and make love, a very potent drug.

SCHULTZ: I would ask Mr. Weinglass please to get on with the trial of this case and stop playing around with raising the Pentagon ten or 300 feet off the ground.

KUNSTLER: Your Honor, this is not playing around. This is a deadly serious business. The whole issue in this case is language, what is meant by saying . . .

SCHULTZ: This is not—this is totally irrelevant.

COURT: Let Mr. Weinglass defend himself.

WEINGLASS: Your Honor, I am glad to see that Mr. Schultz finally concedes that things like levitating the Pentagon building, putting

LSD in the water, nominating a pig for president are all playing around. I am willing to concede that fact, that it was all playing around; it was a play idea of the witness, and if he is willing to concede it we can all go home. Because Mr. Schultz is treating all these things as deadly serious.

SCHULTZ: Did you see some people urinate on the Pentagon?

HOFFMAN: On the Pentagon itself?

SCHULTZ: Or at the Pentagon?

HOFFMAN: In that general area of Washington?

SCHULTZ: Yes.

HOFFMAN: There were in all over 100,000 people. That is, people have that biological habit.

SCHULTZ: And did you?

HOFFMAN: Yes.

SCHULTZ: Did you symbolically?

HOFFMAN: Did I go and look?

SCHULTZ: Did you—did you symbolically urinate on the Pentagon, Mr. Hoffman?

HOFFMAN: I symbolically urinate on the Pentagon?

SCHULTZ: Yes

HOFFMAN: Nearby, yes, in the bushes there, maybe 3,000 feet away from the Pentagon. I didn't get that close. Pee on the walls of the Pentagon? You're getting to be out of sight, actually. Do you think there is a law against it?

SCHULTZ: Are you done, Mr. Hoffman?

HOFFMAN: I am done when you are.

SCHULTZ: Did you ever on a prior occasion state that a sense of integration possesses you and comes from pissing on the Pentagon?

HOFFMAN: What I said was that from combining political attitudes with biological necessity, there is a sense of integration, yes. I think I said it that way, not the way you said it.

SCHULTZ: You had a good time at the Pentagon, didn't you, Mr. Hoffman?

HOFFMAN: Yes, I did. I am having a good time now. In fact, I'm starting to feel that biological necessity right now. Could I be excused for a brief recess?

COURT: We will take a brief recess, ladies and gentlemen of the jury.

HOFFMAN: Just a brief . . .

COURT: We will take a brief recess with my usual orders. A very brief recess.

Blackout.

SCENE FOUR
Testimony of Defense Witness ALLEN GINSBERG

WEINGLASS: Mr. Ginsberg, calling your attention to the month of February 1968, did you have any occasion in that month to meet with Abbie Hoffman?

GINSBERG: Yeah.

WEINGLASS: Do you recall what Mr. Hoffman said in the course of that meeting?

GINSBERG: "Yippee!" Among other things. He said that politics had become theater and magic, that it was the manipulation of imagery through the mass media that was confusing and hypnotizing the people in the United States and making them accept a war that they did not really believe in, that people were involved in a lifestyle that was intolerable to younger folk, which involved brutality and police violence as well as the larger violence in Vietnam. And that ourselves might be able to get together in Chicago and invite teachers to present different ideas about what is wrong with the planet, what we can do to solve the pollution crisis, what we can do to solve the Vietnam War. To present different ideas to make society more sacred, less commercial, less materialistic, what we could do to up-level or improve the whole tone of the trap we all felt ourselves in as the population grew, and as politics became more and more violent and chaotic.

WEINGLASS: After he spoke to you, what if any, was your response to his suggestions?

GINSBERG: I was worried as to whether or not the whole scene would get violent. I was worried whether, you know, the government would let us do something that was funnier, or prettier, or more charming than what was going to be going on in the Convention Hall.

FORAN: I ask that statement be stricken; it was not responsive.

COURT: I sustain the objection.

GINSBERG: Sir, that was our conversation.

COURT: I direct the jury to disregard the last answer of the witness.

WEINGLASS: Your Honor, I would like to be informed by the Court how that answer was not responsive to that question. It seemed to me directly responsive.

FORAN: Your Honor, he asked him what he said and he answered by saying what he was wondering.

GINSBERG: Oh, I am sorry then. I said to Abbie that I was worried about violence.

COURT: I have ruled on the objection. Ask another question if you like.

WEINGLASS: Did you hear Jerry Rubin make a speech in Lincoln Park on August 24th?

GINSBERG: Yes. Jerry Rubin said that he didn't think that it would be a good thing to fight with the police over that eleven o'clock curfew.

WEINGLASS: At approximately ten thirty that evening what was happening in the park?

GINSBERG: There were several thousand young people gathered, waiting. It was dark; there were some bonfires burning in trashcans. Everybody was standing around not knowing what to do. Then, there was a sudden burst of light in the center of the park and a group of policemen moved in fast and kicked over the bonfires.

WEINGLASS: What did you do when you observed the police doing this?

GINSBERG: I started the chant "Ommmmm."

DEFENDANTS: Ommmmm.

FORAN: All right, we have had a demonstration.

COURT: All right.

FORAN: From here on I object.

COURT: You haven't said you objected.

FORAN: I do after the second one.

COURT: After two of them? I sustain the objection.

FORAN: I have no objection to the two Oms we have had. However, I just didn't want to go on all morning.

COURT: Mr. Feinglass, will you please continue with the questioning of this witness?

KUNSTLER: Your Honor, so the record may be clear. I don't think Mr. Weinglass noticed the "Feinglass." (*The Yippies hold up a sheet of paper on which they have written* "WEINGLASS.")

COURT: Oh, I did misspeak myself. I inserted an F there instead of the W you deserve, Mr. Weinglass. Mr. Weinglass. Somebody held up the name.

KUNSTLER: We have the name here, Your Honor.

COURT: Yes.

HOFFMAN: Here it is. Shall we put it on him?

COURT: Yes, yes. Please continue . . .

WEINGLASS: Now Mr. Ginsberg, where if anywhere did you go on Tuesday night, August 27?

GINSBERG: The group I was with, Jean Genet, William Burroughs, and Terry Southern, all went back to Lincoln Park.

WEINGLASS: What was occurring in the park as you got there?

GINSBERG: There was a great crowd lining the outskirts of the park, and at the center of the park there was a group of ministers and rabbis who had elevated a great cross about ten feet high in the middle of a circle of people who were sitting around quietly, listening to the ministers conduct a ceremony.

William Burroughs, Allen Ginsberg, Jean Genet and others, Chicago, 1968.

WEINGLASS: After the ceremony was over, what, if anything, occurred?

GINSBERG: The ministers lifted up the cross and took it to the edge of the crowd and set it down facing the lights where the police were. In other words, they confronted the police lines with the cross of Christ.

WEINGLASS: After the ministers moved the cross to the other location, which you have just indicated, what happened?

GINSBERG: After, I don't know, a short period of time, there was a burst of smoke and tear gas 'round the cross and the cross was enveloped in tear gas and the people who were carrying the cross were enveloped in tear gas, which slowly began drifting over the crowd.

WEINGLASS: And when you saw the persons with the cross and the cross being gassed, what if anything did you do?

GINSBERG: I turned to Burroughs and said, "They have gassed the cross of Christ."

FORAN: Objection, if the Court please. I ask the answer be stricken.

COURT: I sustain the objection.

WEINGLASS: Without relating what you said, Mr. Ginsberg, what did you do at that time?

GINSBERG: I took Bill Burroughs' hand and took Terry Southern's hand and we turned from the cross, which was covered with gas in the glaring lights that were coming from the police lights that were shining through the teargas on the cross, and walked slowly out of the park.

WEINGLASS: Thank you. Nothing further.

COURT: You may cross-examine, Mr. Foran.

FORAN: Mr. Ginsberg, you've been named a sort of religious leader of the Yippies, and you testified concerning a number of books of poetry that you have written?

GINSBERG: Yes.

FORAN: In *The Empty Mirror*, there is a poem called "The Night Apple"?

GINSBERG: Yes.

FORAN: Would you recite that for the jury?

GINSBERG: "The Night Apple."

> Last night I dreamed
> of one I loved
> for seven long years,
> but I saw no face,
> only the familiar
> presence of the body;
> sweat skin eyes
> feces urine sperm
> saliva all one
> odor and mortal taste.

FORAN: Could you explain to the jury, having said that, what the religious significance of that poem is?

GINSBERG: I could, if you would take a wet dream as a religious experience. It is a description of a wet dream, sir.

FORAN: Now, Mr. Ginsberg, you testified when you met Abbie Hoffman in Lincoln Park, you said when you met him you kissed him?

GINSBERG: Yes.

FORAN: Is he an intimate friend of yours?

GINSBERG: I felt very intimate with him. I saw he was struggling to manifest a beautiful thing, and I felt very good towards him.

FORAN: And do you consider him an intimate friend of yours?

GINSBERG: I don't see him that often, but I do see him often enough and have worked with him often enough to feel intimate with him, yes.

FORAN: You feel pretty much an intimate friend of Jerry Rubin's, too?

GINSBERG: Over the years, I have learned from them both.

FORAN: Your Honor, I have to get some materials to properly carry on my cross-examination of this witness. It will take me some time to go downstairs to get them.

COURT: How long will it take?

FORAN: I think at least several minutes, Your Honor. Ten, fifteen minutes.

COURT: Are you suggesting we recess?

FORAN: I would think possibly, yes, Your Honor, because I would just get back here and get started . . .

COURT: You mean recess until the afternoon?

FORAN: After lunch.

COURT: All right. We will go until two o'clock.

WEINGLASS: Your Honor . . .

KUNSTLER: Your Honor, we have witnesses leaving the country this afternoon who are presently here. One is leaving tomorrow morning and must testify now or we lose him forever, and the other has to return to the West Coast.

COURT: I have granted the request of the Prosecution.

KUNSTLER: We asked for five minutes two days ago in front of this jury and you refused to give it to us.

COURT: You will cease to have this disrespectful tone.

KUNSTLER: That is not disrespectful; that is an angry tone, Your Honor.

COURT: Yes, it is. I will grant the motion of the Government.

KUNSTLER: You refused us five minutes the other day. Why the different treatment?

COURT: I will not sit here and have you assume that disrespectful tone to the Court.

KUNSTLER: This is not disrespectful.

COURT: Yes, it is.

KUNSTLER: I am asking you to explain to the Defense, which claims it is getting different treatment, why a simple request for five minutes was not granted.

COURT: I have admonished you time and again to be respectful to the Court. I have been respectful to you.

KUNSTLER: Your Honor, this is not disrespectful to anybody but . . .

COURT: You are shouting at the Court.

KUNSTLER: Oh, Your Honor.

COURT: Shouting at the Court the way you do.

KUNSTLER: Everyone has shouted from time to time, including Your Honor. This is not a situation . . .

COURT: Make a note of that. I have never . . .

KUNSTLER: Voices have been raised.

COURT: I have never shouted at you during this trial.

KUNSTLER: Your Honor, your voice has been raised.

COURT: You have been disrespectful.

KUNSTLER: It is not disrespectful, Your Honor.

COURT: And sometimes worse than that.

GINSBERG: Ommmmmm.

(The judge uses his gavel.)

KUNSTLER: He was trying to calm us down, Your Honor.

COURT: Oh, no! I need no calming down.

Blackout.

SCENE FIVE
Examination of Defense Witness RICHARD DALEY
Mayor of Chicago

KUNSTLER: Mayor Daley, in one of your answers to my previous questions you stated something about your instructions to offer hospitality to people coming to Chicago.

FORAN: I object to the form of the question, Your Honor, as leading.

KUNSTLER: It's not even a question, Your Honor. It's a statement, a predicate for . . .

COURT: Well, ask the question. Don't summarize the previous evidence. I sustain the objection.

KUNSTLER: In view of what you said, do you consider the use of nightsticks on the heads of demonstrators was hospitable?

FORAN: Objection, Your Honor.

COURT: I sustain the objection.

KUNSTLER: Mayor Daley, do you believe that people have a right to demonstrate against the war in Vietnam?

FORAN: Your Honor, I object to the form of the question. It is an improper form of question.

COURT: I sustain the objection to the question.

KUNSTLER: Mayor Daley, on 28th of August 1968, did you say to Senator Ribicoff . . .

FORAN: Oh, Your Honor, I object.

KUNSTLER: "Fuck you, you Jew son-of-a-bitch, you lousy motherfucker, go home"?

FORAN: Of all the improper, foolish questions—typical, Your Honor, of making up questions that have nothing to do with the lawsuit.

KUNSTLER: That is not a made-up question, Your Honor. We can prove that.

FORAN: I ask that counsel be admonished, Your Honor.

KUNSTLER: I have the source, Your Honor.

COURT: May I suggest to you, sir, that this witness is your witness and you may not ask him any leading questions even of the sort that you proposed—especially rather of the sort that I heard part of a moment ago.

KUNSTLER: Your Honor, I have tried to reiterate ten times that in view of the nature of this witness, it is impossible to examine him and get the truth of the matter with these restrictions . . .

COURT: This witness is no different from any other witness.

KUNSTLER: But, Your Honor, that isn't so. He is different from any other witness. He is the mayor of the city . . .

COURT: In this court he is just another witness.

KUNSTLER: Well, Your Honor, then I renew my motion that he be declared a hostile witness.

WEINGLASS: Your Honor, Rule 43(b), Federal Rule of Civil Procedure, states that a party may interrogate any unwilling hostile witness by leading questions as if he had been called by the adverse party.

COURT: The motion will be denied. The Court finds that there is nothing in the testimony of the witness that has indicated hostility. On the contrary, his manner has been that of a gentleman.

KUNSTLER: But, Your Honor, the defendants have publicly stated that they believe that he is the real culprit here.

COURT: You procured him to come to a court through a writ that was issued out of this Court. He is here. If you ask him the proper questions . . .

KUNSTLER: We are trying, Your Honor, to get to the truth of what happened during Convention Week.

COURT: You must get at the truth through proper questions, sir.

FORAN: Through the law of evidence, Your Honor, that it has taken five hundred years to achieve.

KUNSTLER: Mayor Daley, have you been at all familiar with the report of President Johnson's Commission to investigate the causes of violence at the Democratic National Convention?

FORAN: I object, Your Honor.

COURT: I sustain the objection.

KUNSTLER: Do you agree with the Commission's finding that a police riot took place in the city of Chicago?

FORAN: Your Honor, I object to that. I ask the jury be instructed to disregard it, and I ask that counsel be admonished for asking an intentionally improper question.

COURT: I sustain the objection because it is grossly improper. I direct the jury to disregard the last question put to the witness by Mr. Kunstler.

SCHULTZ: But, Your Honor, there is a problem here. Most of the questions are leading, and we don't object to all of them, but we keep on getting up and getting up. As I said before, it becomes embarrassing . . . for people who don't know the legal rules, it looks very bad for the Government to be constantly getting up. It makes it appear that we are trying to hide certain things, and we just want him to conform to the proper line of questioning.

KUNSTLER: Your Honor, is this an objection or a speech, because we don't understand it.

SCHULTZ: I am begging defense counsel to ask questions properly.

COURT: Don't beg.

SCHULTZ: That is what it is, Your Honor.

COURT: Don't beg. You needn't beg. I will order them not to ask leading questions. I order you not to ask any leading questions.

Blackout.

SCENE SIX
Examination of Defense Witness DONALD PETERSON
Chairman of the Wisconsin Delegation to the 1968 *Democratic Convention*

WEINGLASS: If the Court's ruling is that anything that occurred on the floor of the convention is irrelevant to this, I have no further questions, but if the Court does not make the ruling, I will attempt to elicit from this witness what occurred on the floor of the convention. I am just asking the Court what the basis of the ruling . . .

COURT: I am not obligated to answer that question.

WEINGLASS: Well then, we will have to go on. Now, I don't want to waste this time.

SCHULTZ: Then let Mr. Weinglass, without asking a leading question, ask the witness what happened on the floor of the convention at about a certain time without suggesting . . .

WEINGLASS: I thought I did that.

SCHULTZ: No, Mr. Weinglass. If he asks that question . . .

WEINGLASS: Okay, I don't want to argue this.

SCHULTZ: I will object to that question. But if he asks it non-leading, then we can resolve Mr. Weinglass's dilemma.

WEINGLASS: Mr. Peterson, what happened on the floor of the convention at approximately ten o'clock?

SCHULTZ: Objection.

COURT: I sustain the objection.

WEINGLASS: That is incredible.

SCHULTZ: Now Mr. Weinglass has the ruling of the Court in this area.

WEINGLASS: Mr. Peterson, what happened on the floor of the convention at approximately ten thirty?

SCHULTZ: Objection, Your Honor.

COURT: I sustain the objection.

WEINGLASS: What happened on the floor at any time that night after nine p.m.?

SCHULTZ: Objection.

COURT: I sustain the objection.

WEINGLASS: Mr. Peterson, what did you do on the floor of the convention?

SCHULTZ: Same objection, Your Honor, relevancy.

COURT: I sustain the objection.

SCHULTZ: Now Mr. Weinglass has the Court's ruling that what happened at the convention on Wednesday night is not material to this case.

Blackout.

SCENE SEVEN
When the court was not in session the defendants were allowed to appear publicly throughout the country to raise money for their defense.

COURT: It has been brought to my notice that there was a speech given in Milwaukee discussing this case by one of the defendants— not that this was the first time a speech was given about this case by one of the defendants in this trial. I want to say that if such a speech as was given is brought to my attention again, I will give consideration to the termination of bail of the person who makes the speech. I think he would be a bad risk to continue on bail. Mr. Marshal, bring in the next witness please.

DELLINGER: I made the speech.

COURT: What did you say?

DELLINGER: I made the speech. Was there anything in the speech that suggested I wouldn't show up for trial the next day, or simply that I criticized your conduct of the trial?

COURT: I didn't ask you to rise, sir, and I am certainly not going to be interrogated.

DELLINGER: Why are you threatening me with revocation of bail for exercising my freedom of speech? What has that got to do with it? I am here, aren't I?

HOFFMAN: Right on.

COURT: I think it is wholly inappropriate for defendants in a criminal case to make the kind of speech that was made, and the matter of bail goes beyond mere protection for the Government that the defendant appear.

HOFFMAN: I will be in Miami on Sunday with the same speech. (*Other* DEFENDANTS *name cities.*)

COURT: Did you hear that? I haven't heard either lawyer for the defendants try to quiet their clients during this trial when they spoke out, not once in four and a half months—not once.

WEINGLASS: This question of bail revocation: I think Your Honor should clarify . . .

COURT: I will determine what to do if and when speeches of a certain kind and character are brought to my attention. Free speech is not at issue here.

Blackout.

SCENE EIGHT
Rebuttal Case for the Government
Testimony of Government Witness JAMES B. HATLEN
Deputy Chief of the Chicago Police

SCHULTZ: Now, at approximately five forty-five, what if any announcements were made?

HATLEN: I heard an unidentified speaker announce over a bullhorn to the group that inasmuch as the march had been stopped, to break in small groups and go over to the Loop, and disrupt their normal activity, and, if possible, to tie up traffic in the Loop.

SCHULTZ: Did the defendant Dellinger say anything when this announcement was completed?

HATLEN: I do not recall him stating anything, but I did notice that he left with the head of the march, with the group that was carrying flags.

DELLINGER: Oh, bullshit.

COURT: Did you get that, Miss Reporter?

DELLINGER: That is an absolute lie.

COURT: Did you get that, Miss Reporter?

DELLINGER: Let's argue about what I stand for and what you stand for, but let's not make up things like that.

COURT: I will not permit the obscenities engaged in or applied by Mr. Dellinger. I don't use that kind of language myself. And I don't even like to use it in court here to quote the defendant. I shall turn over a transcript to the United States Attorney, and I hereby terminate the bail of the defendant Dellinger and remand him to the custody of the United States Marshal for the Northern District of Illinois for the remainder of this trial.

KUNSTLER: He is my client and I think this is utterly . . .

COURT: This isn't the first word and I won't argue this.

DELLINGER: There's no pretense of fairness in this court.

MARSHAL: Be quiet, sir.

DELLINGER: You gagged Bobby Seale because you couldn't afford to listen to the truth that he was saying to you. Now you're accusing me . . .

MARSHAL: Sit down please, and be quiet. Will you be quiet, Mr. Dellinger?

DAVIS: This court is bullshit.

COURT: There he is saying the same words again.

HAYDEN: You can jail the revolutionary but you can't jail the revolution. (DELLINGER *is knocked to the floor by the* MARSHALS, *and a courtroom battle ensues.*)

DAVIS: No, I say it. Everything in this court is bullshit. I associate myself with David Dellinger completely, 100 percent. This is the most obscene court I have ever seen.

HOFFMAN: You know you can't win this fucking case. The only way you can is to put us away for contempt. We have contempt for this court and for this whole rotten system. That is why they want this, because they can't prove this fucking case.

COURT: Mr. Marshal, will you ask defendant Hoffman to sit down.

HOFFMAN: Oh, tell him to stuff it up his bowling ball. How's your war stock doing, Julie?

Blackout.

SCENE NINE
Closing Arguments

SCHULTZ: Ladies and gentlemen of the jury, gentlemen of the Defense. The Government rested its case over two months ago, and it is hard to remember what all that evidence was, especially when the defendants never met the Government's case. So there was nothing to refresh you as to what the issues were, because in the last two months you have hardly heard a scrap of evidence that relates to the case, to the charges in the indictment.

WEINGLASS: Ladies and gentlemen of the jury. The Government has to prove its case beyond a reasonable doubt, and you have to believe it beyond a reasonable doubt, and if you can believe the starting premise of the Government's case, that these men plotted to put themselves in jail, that they conspired to have this trial, then you could find them guilty. But I suggest to you that the whole foundation upon which this case is built, the whole structure of it, put in terms of common sense, is just not acceptable as a rational proposition.

SCHULTZ: Now the first question you must ask yourselves is why would anybody want to incite a riot. Why would anybody want to incite a situation where people are beating each other, where demonstrators are beating policemen, policemen are beating demonstrators. Why would they want this? Well, in answering this question we can look at the defendants' own statements. Davis wanted the president to use troops to secure the nomination. He wanted to use violence to precipitate the National Liberation Front in the United States. Where people would rise up in anger against the government, and that would be precipitated by a riot. Hayden wanted to create what he referred to after the convention as the first step towards the revolution. Dellinger said he wanted to bring the U.S. military machinery to a halt. Rubin. Rubin told Norman Mailer in December 1967 that the presence of 100,000 people at the Festival of Life would so terrify the establishment that the convention would be held under armed guard, and the resulting violence by the establishment itself would be such that the establishment would smash the city. Hoffman stated right after the convention that he wanted to smash this system by any means at his disposal. He stated in an interview that was published that he wanted "to wreck this fucking society." That's what he said. So while the defendants profess that they came here for nonviolence, their own statements contradict that.

WEINGLASS: Abbie Hoffman and Rennie Davis signed their names to applications in one case five months before the convention. Abbie flew here three times to meet with city officials. Rennie is here constantly meeting with them. And when they couldn't get what they wanted, what did they do, these men who wanted all this violence? They filed a lawsuit in this building, in the Federal Courthouse compelling the city that won't negotiate with them to come to court. And all this, the Government would have you believe, these men did while they intended to cause violence and a civil disturbance in this city.

SCHULTZ: They are guilty of coming here to incite a riot. They came here and they incited a riot.

WEINGLASS: I want to indicate to you in closing that this case is more than just the defense of seven men. It involves the more basic issue of whether or not those who dare to stand up can do so in this country without grave personal risk, and I think it will be judged in that light. And I think while you deliberate on this case, that history will hold its breath until you determine whether or not this wrong we have been living with will be righted by a verdict of acquittal for the seven men who are on trial here. Thank you.

COURT: Mr. Foran . . .

FORAN: Ladies and gentleman of the jury. These are highly sophisticated, highly educated men, every one of them. They are not kids. Davis, the youngest, is twenty-nine. These are highly sophisticated, educated men, and they are evil men. There are millions of kids who naturally resent authority, who are impatient for change, want to fix things up. There is another thing about a kid, if we all remember— that you have an attraction to evil. Evil is exciting and evil is interesting, and plenty of kids have a fascination for it. These men know how to draw the kids together and use them to accomplish their purposes. Kids in the '60s are disillusioned. They feel that John Kennedy went, Bobby Kennedy went, Martin Luther King went, and the kids do feel that the lights have gone out in Camelot, the banners are furled, and the parade is over. These guys take advantage of them, evilly, and they use them for their purposes. They tried to give us this bunk that they wanted to talk about racism and the war, and they wanted a counter-convention. They didn't do anything but look for a confrontation with the police.

KUNSTLER: We are living in extremely troubled times. An intolerable war abroad has divided us; racism and poverty at home are both causes of despair and discouragement. In a so-called affluent society, we have people starving and people who can't even begin to approximate a decent life. These are terrible problems, but they don't go away by destroying their critics. They don't vanish by sending men to jail. They never did and they never will.

FORAN: Of course, the imperfections of our life cry out for answers. They cry out for legal answers. Effective law is the greatest achievement of mankind yet, and I believe most Americans feel it is not only necessary but is highly desirable. We must have law. The vision and ideals of our forefathers cannot be corrupted by the haters and the violent anarchists. The lights in Camelot that kids believe in need not go out. These banners can snap in the spring breeze, and the parade will never be over if people will remember what Thomas Jefferson said: "Obedience to the law is the major part of patriotism." These seven men have been proven guilty beyond any doubt. You are under oath to fulfill your obligation without fear, favor, or sympathy. Do your duty.

COURT: In reaching your verdict you must not in any way be influenced by any possible antagonisms you may have towards the defendants—their dress, hairstyles, speech, reputation, courtroom behavior or quality, personal philosophy, or lifestyle.

SCENE TEN

The Contempt Citations

All the defendants, as well as their lawyers, were sentenced for
contempt of court.

COURT: From the outset of the trial, the court admonished and warned the defendants and their counsel to refrain from such conduct, particularly when committed in the presence of the jury. They chose deliberately to disregard such admonitions and have openly challenged and flaunted their contempt for both this court and the system of law it represents. Particularly reprehensible was the conduct of counsel, who not only disregarded a duty to advise and direct their clients to observe the rules of this court, but participated with their clients in making a mockery of orderly procedure.

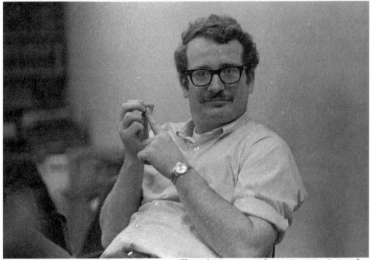

John Froines at defense attorneys' offices during pretrial meetings, spring 1969.

NACIO JAN BROWN

The defendant JOHN FROINES *is sentenced to six months and eight*
days for contempt.

FROINES: No, Your Honor! There are millions of defendants through-out this country who still have to be charged. And neither you, nor anybody like you can punish and sentence all of them. When history is written, the men who are sitting at this table, and the people in the spectator section who stood all night to get into this courtroom, they are the heroes. What's going to happen in this country is something that a man like you couldn't possibly understand.

COURT: Crowd out of your minds that this Court ever set out to be a hero. Any judge who sets out to be a hero or all things to all people, well, he'll be a mighty incompetent judge.

FROINES: I'm not suggesting that you're a hero, so you don't have to deny it.

COURT: No man in his profession may be perfect, but you and your codefendants have availed yourselves of the benefits of the American federal judiciary system.

FROINES: Availed ourselves. You have that a little bit backwards, don't you? Because we didn't ask to come here.

COURT: What did you say?

FROINES: We didn't ask to come here. I would have preferred to stay where I was.

Lee Weiner at defense attorneys' offices during pretrial meetings, spring 1969.

The defendant LEE WEINER *is sentenced to two months and seventeen days for contempt.*

WEINER: Throughout this trial I have sat in quiet rage over what I've seen go on in this courtroom. If I didn't stand four times and that constitutes contempt of court—I can only say to you that I feel that contempt of court very deeply, very strongly in my heart, and yet I don't personally condemn you for being what you are, just as I don't personally condemn Tom or Dicky. They are technicians: they do their job for a fascist state.

COURT: I must admonish you, sir . . .

WEINER: Yes, you must admonish me . . .

COURT: I am supposed to be especially tolerant, because years ago when I was a much younger man, I was a member of the faculty of the school that you—I don't know whether you still are—at least it has been suggested here during this trial that you are or were a teacher there.

WEINER: I even understand that there is a plaque naming an auditorium after you at the Law School. At latest report, by the way . . .

COURT: You are nice to tell the assembled spectators here . . .

WEINER: I tell them actually for an evil reason . . .

COURT: . . .that there is a Hoffman Hall on Northwestern University's campus.

WEINER: I tell them actually because I am suggesting it is evil.

COURT: Yes, well, perhaps those who think ill of me here because of some of the things that have been said might have some compassion.

WEINER: I'm pleased to inform you that the plaque has been ripped off the wall.

COURT: My plaque?

WEINER: Your plaque has been ripped off the wall in the auditorium. You see, apparently while the Board of Trustees has this great affection for you, the student body does not.

The defendant DAVID DELLINGER *is sentenced to two years, five months, and sixteen days for contempt.*

COURT: The Court has concluded its reading of the record in respect to the defendant Dellinger. The Court finds defendant Dellinger guilty of direct contempt of court. Mr. Dellinger, do you care to say anything before sentence is imposed?

DELLINGER: Yes.

COURT: Not a legal argument.

DELLINGER: No. I want to make a statement on the context . . .

COURT: Only in respect to punishment, I will hear you.

DELLINGER: Yes. I think it relates—and I hope you will do me the courtesy not to interrupt me while I am talking.

COURT: I won't interrupt as long as you are respectful.

DELLINGER: Well, I will talk about the facts, and the facts don't always encourage false respect. Now, I want to point out first of all that the first two contempts cited against me concerned one, the moratorium action and, secondly, support of Bobby Seale. The war against Vietnam, the aggression against Vietnam, and racism in this country, are two issues that this country refuses to take seriously.

COURT: I hope you will excuse me, sir. You are not speaking strictly to what I gave you the privilege of speaking to. I asked you to say what you want in respect to punishment.

DELLINGER: I think this relates to the punishment.

COURT: Get to the subject of punishment and I will be glad to hear you. I don't want you to talk politics.

DELLINGER: You see, that's one of the reasons I have needed to stand up and speak here, because you have tried to keep what you call politics, which means the truth, out of this courtroom, just as the Prosecution has.

COURT: I will ask you to sit down.

DELLINGER: Therefore, it is necessary . . .

COURT: I won't let you go any further.

DELLINGER: You wanted us to be like the good Germans supporting the evils of our decade, and then when we refused to be good Germans and came to Chicago and demonstrated, despite the threats and intimidations of the establishment, now you want us to be like good Jews, going quietly and politely to the concentration camps while you and this Court suppress freedom and truth. Well, the fact is, I am not prepared to do that. You want us to stay in our place like black people are supposed to—stay in their place . . .

COURT: Mr. Marshal, I will ask you to have Mr. Dellinger sit down.

DELLINGER: . . . like poor people are supposed to stay in their place, like people without formal education are supposed to stay in their place, like women are supposed to stay in their place . . .

COURT: I will ask you to sit down.

DELLINGER: . . . like children are supposed to stay in their place, like lawyers are supposed to stay in their places.

MARSHAL: Be quiet, Mr. Dellinger.

DELLINGER: You take an hour to read the contempt citation, you have the power to send me away for years, but you will not give me one tenth the time to speak what is relevant by my desserts and by history's desserts as well. I sat here and heard that man, Mr. Foran, say evil, terrible, dishonest things that even he could not believe in—I heard him say that, and you expect me to be quiet and accept that without speaking up.

People will no longer be quiet. People are going to speak up. I am an old man, and I am just speaking feebly and not too well, but I reflect the spirit that will echo throughout the world.

COURT: Take him out.

DELLINGER'S DAUGHTER: Daddy, daddy!

DELLINGER: Leave my daughter alone. Leave my daughter alone.

DELLINGER'S DAUGHTER: Daddy, daddy . . . !

DEFENDANT: Leave that girl alone.

DEFENDANT: Leave her alone.

MARSHAL: Will everyone sit down?

SPECTATOR: Get your fucking storm troopers out of here.

MARSHAL: All right, sit down. Have a seat!

SPECTATORS: (*Offstage.*) The whole world is watching! The whole world is watching!

DELLINGER: Well, you preserved law and order here today, Judge. The day will come when you'll take every one of us.

Blackout.

SCENE ELEVEN
Verdicts and Sentencing
February 18, 1970

"If we make nonviolent revolution impossible, we make violent revolution inevitable."
—John F. Kennedy

COURT: Good morning, ladies and gentlemen of the jury. I am informed by the United States Marshal that you have reached a verdict or some verdicts. I direct the clerk to read the verdicts.

CLERK: Defendant Abbott H. Hoffman has been found guilty as charged.

COURT: Mr. Hoffman, do you have anything to say before sentencing is imposed?

HOFFMAN: Oh, yeah. I feel like I have spent fifteen years watching

"You Are There." It's sort of like taking LSD, which I recommend to you, Judge. I know a good dealer in Miami. I could fix you up.

DELLINGER: I feel more compassion for you, sir, than I do any hostility. I feel that you are a man who has had too much power over the lives of too many people for too many years. You have sentenced them to degrading conditions without being fully aware of what you are doing, and undoubtedly feeling correct and righteous, as often happens when people do the most abominable things.

RUBIN: You have done more to destroy the court system in this country than any of us could have ever done. All we did was come to Chicago, and the police system exposed itself as totalitarian. All we did is walk into the courtroom, and the court system exposed itself as totalitarian.

HOFFMAN: Mr. Foran says that we're unpatriotic. Unpatriotic. I don't know, that has a kind of a jingoistic ring. I suppose I am not patriotic. But he says we are un-American. I don't feel un-American. I feel very American. I said it's not that the Yippies hate America. It is that the American dream has been betrayed. That has been my attitude.

DAVIS: When I come out of prison, it will be to move next door to Tom Foran. I am going to be the boy next door to Tom Foran. And the boy next door, the boy that could have been a judge, could have been a prosecutor, could have been a college professor, is going to move next door to organize his kids into the revolution!

DELLINGER: Our movement is not very strong today. It is not united, it is not well organized; it is very confused and makes a lot of mistakes. But there is the beginning of an awakening in this country that will

Jerry Rubin at defense attorneys' offices during pretrial meetings, spring 1969.

not be denied, because however falsely applied the American ideal was from the beginning, nonetheless there was a dream of justice, equality, freedom, and brotherhood, and I think that dream is much closer to fulfillment today than it has been at any time in the history of this country.

HOFFMAN: I know those guys on the wall. I know them better than you; I feel I know Adams—I mean, I know all the Adamses. They grew up 20 miles from my home in Massachusetts. I played with Sam Adams on the Concord Bridge. I was there when Paul Revere rode right up on his motorcycle and said, "The pigs are coming; the pigs are coming!" I was there. I know the Adamses. Sam Adams was an evil man.

RUBIN: I am glad we exposed the court system, because in millions of courthouses across this country blacks are being shuttled from the streets to the jails and nobody knows about it. They're forgotten men.

You see, what we've done is, we've exposed that. Maybe now people will be interested in what happens in the courthouse down the street because of what happened here.

COURT: I sentence you to five years imprisonment, $5,000 fine, and the cost of prosecution.

HOFFMAN: Jefferson. Thomas Jefferson called for a revolution every ten years. Jefferson had an agrarian reform program that made Mao Tse-tung look like a liberal. I know Thomas Jefferson.

DAVIS: We are going to turn the sons and daughters of the ruling class of this country into Viet Cong.

COURT: I sentence you to five years imprisonment, $5,000 fine, and the cost of prosecution.

HOFFMAN: Washington. Washington grew pot. He called it hemp. It was called hemp then. He probably was a pothead.

DELLINGER: I only wish that we were all not just eloquent. I wish we were smarter, more dedicated, more united. I wish we could all work together. I wish we could reach out to the Forans and the Schultzes and the Hoffmans, and convince them of the necessity of this revolution.

COURT: I sentence you to five years imprisonment, a $5,000 fine, and the costs of prosecution.

HOFFMAN: Abraham Lincoln? There's another one. In 1861, Abraham Lincoln in his inaugural address said, and I quote, "When the people shall grow weary of their constitutional right to amend the government, they shall exert their revolutionary right to dismember and overthrow that government." Now, if Abraham Lincoln had given that speech in Lincoln Park, he would be on trial right here in this courtroom, because that is an inciteful speech. That is a speech intended to create a riot!

HAYDEN: The problem for those who seek to punish is that the punishment doesn't have the desired effect. Even as Dellinger is taken off to jail for his justified contempt of this court, his teenage daughter jumps up and fights back. The punishment only fuels the protest. So, Your Honor, before your eyes you see the most vital ingredient of your system collapsing, because the system does not hold together.

COURT: Oh, don't be so pessimistic. Our system isn't collapsing. And fellows as smart as you could do awfully well under this system. I am not trying to convert you, mind you.

HOFFMAN: We don't want a place in the regiment, Julie.

COURT: What did you say? Your sentencing is coming up.

HOFFMAN: I'm being patient, Julie.

COURT: Well, I don't—you see? He thinks that annoys me by addressing me by a name—he doesn't know that years ago, when I was his age or younger, that's what my friends called me.

HAYDEN: The point I was trying to make is that I was trying to think about what I regretted and about punishment. I can only state one thing that affected my feelings, my own feelings, and that is that I would like to have a child.

COURT: That is where the federal system can do you no good.

HAYDEN: Because the federal system can do you no good in trying to prevent the birth of a new world!

HOFFMAN: I don't even know what a riot is, I thought a riot was fun. Riot means you laugh: ha-ha. That's a riot. They call it a riot. I didn't want to be that serious. I was supposed to be funny. Well, it wasn't funny last night sitting in my prison cell, a five-by-eight room, with no light in it—nothing. Bedbugs all over. They bite. I haven't eaten in six days. I'm not on a hunger strike; you can call it a hunger strike. It's just that the food stinks and I can't take it.

HAYDEN: We would hardly be notorious characters if they had left us alone in the streets of Chicago last year. It would have been a few thousand people. It would have been a testimony to our failure as organizers. But instead we became the architects, the masterminds and the geniuses of a conspiracy to overthrow the government. We were invented. We were chosen by the government to serve as scapegoats for all they wanted to prevent happening in the 1970s. We were chosen because we had a history in the 1960s of doing things that had to be stopped. If you didn't want to make us martyrs, why did you do it? You know if you had given us a permit, you know if you had given slightly different instructions, very little would have happened last year in Chicago.

COURT: I sentence you to five years in prison, a $5,000 fine, and costs of prosecution.

HOFFMAN: Well, we said it was like Alice in Wonderland coming in, now I feel like Alice in 1984, because I have lived through the winter of injustice in this trial.

COURT: The defendant Abbott H. Hoffman will be committed to the custody of the Attorney General for imprisonment for a term of five years. Further, a fine of $5,000 and costs . . .

HOFFMAN: $5,000, Judge? Could you make that $350?

COURT: $5,000 and . . .

HOFFMAN: How about $3.50?

COURT: . . .and costs will be imposed, costs of prosecution will be imposed. Mr. Marshal . . .

HOFFMAN: Remember to water the plants.

CLERK: The defendant Lee Weiner is found not guilty as charged. The defendant John R. Froines is found not guilty as charged.

COURT: The defendants stand committed until the fine and the costs have been paid, the prison terms to run consecutively with the prison term or prison sentence previously imposed for direct contempt of court. Not only the record in this case, covering a period of four months or longer, but from the remarks made by the defendants themselves here today, the Court finds that the defendants are clearly dangerous people to be at large. Therefore the commitments here will be without bail. (KUNSTLER *rises.*) I gave you the opportunity to speak at the very beginning. You said counsel did not desire to speak.

KUNSTLER: Your Honor, couldn't I say my last words without you cutting me off?

COURT: You said you had nothing to say.

KUNSTLER: Your Honor, I said just a moment ago we had a concluding remark. Your Honor has succeeded perhaps in sullying it, and I think that maybe that is the way the case should end, as it began.

Final blackout.

Jerry Rubin, Abbie Hoffman and Tom Hayden (holding microphone) at a press conference, spring 1969. NACIO JAN BROWN

II.

Chicago: 1968–1970

by Tom Hayden

THE VIOLENCE OF SPRING

As 1968 began, I felt I was living on the knife edge of history. It did, of course, turn out to be a year of extraordinary turmoil, a climax to events that had begun five years earlier with the assassination of President Kennedy, when for the first time someone central to our national life was brutally and publicly eliminated. The killing of leaders became a legitimized part of our normalcy. The places I lived in those times—Atlanta, Newark, then Chicago—cemented the status quo with coercion and violence. But now, in 1968, a massive and continuous system malfunction occurred.

The power elite, which C. Wright Mills had portrayed as invincible, was under siege on all sides. The Tet offensive, student uprisings, Lyndon Johnson's decision not to run for a second term, and the killings of Martin Luther King and Robert F. Kennedy led to a meltdown of the system's core. The breakdown happened not only in Chicago, not only in America; in some mysterious way, it was a global phenomenon. Like a Greek drama, it started with legendary events, then raised hopes, only to end by immersing innocence in tragedy—an experience, for those who went through it all, felt to this day in failed dreams, enduring hurts, unmet yearnings.

I began that year still living in Newark but planning to move to Chicago, where, with Rennie Davis, I would serve as codirector of the projected protests at the Democratic National Convention. Not only was Chicago the tough heartland of America, it was, coincidentally, the national headquarters of Students for a Democratic Society (SDS). The organization had moved there to be in "Middle America." SDS leaders like Rennie, Todd Gitlin, Nanci Hollander, Leni Zeiger, and my former wife Casey (who had left the Student Nonviolent Coordinating Committee in 1966) had worked in the ERAP project among poor whites on Chicago's North Side. Sharon Jeffrey was directing the Woodlawn Organization, a powerful neighborhood organization, and Richie and Vivian Rothstein had migrated to a middle-class suburb, where they were organizing around school issues. Paul Booth, as ever, was working to reform the Democratic Party. Dick Flacks and Bob Ross were budding sociologists at the University of Chicago, while actively building the New University Conference (NUC), which they saw as an academic wing of the movement.

Chicago, under Mayor Richard Daley, was a difficult city to reform in any way. Backed by rabidly conservative editorials in the *Chicago Tribune*, the Daley machine treated critics as mortal enemies and employed all forms of harassment against them. Martin Luther King's 1966 struggle to break down the city's rigid segregation, including the march through Cicero and rallies of 50,000 at Soldier Field, had failed, and the black leader was denounced by Mayor Daley for "creating trouble in every city he visited." The ERAP project was raided and disrupted by the police's "Red Squad," who planted drugs and hypodermic needles on the premises.

In response to the riots after King's murder in April, the *Chicago Tribune* declared, "Here in Chicago we are not dealing with the colored population but with a minority of criminal scum" and urged Daley not to behave like the "spineless and indecisive mayors who muffed early riot control" in Newark and Los Angeles. Three days later, on April 10, the *Tribune* accused Rennie of being the conspiratorial instigator of a plan to turn a King peace memorial service into a violent uprising, stating, "It is an outrage that this country has to deal with a second front at home against rioters and beatniks when the fighting men are risking death overseas."

It was later established that *Tribune* writers cooperated with the FBI in preparing their coverage of SDS.

Nevertheless, activists in Chicago and around the country were expectantly discussing a mass action in Daley's town. The previous year's escalating protests against the draft in Oakland, at the Pentagon, and at New York's Whitehall Induction Center had triggered a magnetic interest in the process of confrontation, in which flower children faced soldiers, shadowy street people threw back tear-gas canisters at police, and bayonets were used to guard democracy. For these militants, the force of logic having failed, the logic of force was fast becoming the only alternative. As Mario Savio, a 1964 Mississippi veteran and the articulate leader of the free-speech movement at Berkeley, had declared two years before: "There is a time when the operation of the machine becomes so odious, makes you so sick at heart, that you can't take part: you can't even tacitly take part, and you've got to put your bodies upon the gears and upon the wheels, upon the levers, upon all the apparatus and you've got to make it stop. And you've got to indicate to the people who run it, to the people who own it, that unless you're free, the machines will be prevented from working at all."

There was also the opposite view that this was the stuff of fantasy, that the only result of such romantic militancy would be the further alienation of Middle America and, quite possibly, repression. This reaction came not only from the older leftist peace groups, but more potently from those committing themselves to working within the political system to "dump Johnson." Senator Eugene McCarthy had announced his antiwar presidential campaign on November 30, 1967, and already thousands of liberal young people were signing on. A frequently bitter debate was triggered among radicals and antiwar activists over whether to be "clean for Gene."

Rennie and I decided to make the most of all these dissident forces. Those with a more radical reading of the American system would "confront the war-makers" in Chicago with a huge demonstration, forcing the Democrats to choose between ending the war and alienating key electoral constituencies. This very confrontation would enhance the arguments of reformers within the party, I predicted, while also keeping the antiwar movement independent and in the streets. I could identify with the idealism and commitment of the McCarthy workers who slept on floors across the country, although I thought Robert Kennedy would be a better candidate. However, if they succeeded against the top-down delegate-selection rules, it would shock me. I drove up to a Yale seminar given by an old friend, Geoff Cowan, who had been active in McComb in 1964 and during the Mississippi Freedom Democratic Party summer challenge at the Democratic convention. Geoff, a McCarthy activist, was angered at the Democratic Party rules that allowed convention delegates to be controlled by party bosses—many of them even before the 1968 primaries began. He was prepared to carry a challenge all the way to the Chicago convention, demanding a share of delegates in proportion to a candidate's vote in primaries. If they failed, as I expected, they would still be a formidable factor in the antiwar movement and at least would have forged a power base for dissent within the Democratic Party.

I felt that our movement's long debate over the nature of American power, started by C. Wright Mills and continued at Port Huron, might be resolved in this election year. Was there a stable power elite above even the president? Could an incumbent president be defeated by an electoral movement? Could the United States be forced to leave Vietnam? Would the elite suspend the democratic process in favor of repression if their interests were too deeply threatened? Or could democracy—not just democracy at the ballot box but democracy in the streets—be an effective antidote to the conspiracies of the state? We would see, through our own experience in history rather than academic speculation.

At the start of the year, the Vietnamese launched their Tet offensive and began imprinting a new legend on our consciousness. When the fires of Tet subsided two months later, the defenders of U.S. policy climbed out of their public-relations bunkers to make the Orwellian claim that the real result was a military defeat for North Vietnam and the NLF, but a psychological setback for the United States because of demoralizing media coverage.

Against these Pentagon morticians with their body-count mentalities, the Vietnamese seemed to me like supermen. They were ruthless, as in the Tet killings of civilians in Hué, but I was awed by their fearless survival under the American military pounding. Their Tet offensive did not overthrow the Saigon government, but it destroyed the U.S. pacification program and shattered any Pentagon illusions about a "light at the end of the tunnel." As the U.S. military turned into a wounded Cyclops stumbling through the rice paddies, fighting to retain besieged outposts like Khe Sanh, the war was becoming what one historian called the "peak folly of an older generation." The weekly American death toll rose to 542, an intolerable high; the generals requested 206,000 more troops, an unacceptable burden; the White House proposed a $32 billion Vietnam budget for 1968–69, an unsustainable cost. The turning point had been reached. Change was in the air.

I spoke to Rennie in Chicago daily during the Tet offensive. He was planning to set up an office for the convention actions which were six months away. The flavor of the rapid-fire discussions went like this:

"Hey, man, is the war over?"

"I don't think so, but this doesn't help Johnson a whole lot, does it? Do you think Kennedy will get in now?"

"I don't know, but I bet he wishes he had. Anyway, what the hell can we plan on? If there's an escalation by Johnson, forget permits and get ready to die in riots at the convention. If there is a de-escalation and peace talks, maybe we lose steam and should reconsider the whole thing."

"You ready out there?"

"Yeah, I'm gettin' my Ho Chi Minh sandals on."

"I'm coming by sampan over Lake Michigan."

"Did you hear the papers said the Yippies will put LSD in the water supply?"

"Oh, great."

"You got it, man. Let's meet. I think we can still convince them that we can control it. I'm talking to the Justice Department about mediating with Daley and getting the permits for us."

After what they considered the Pentagon's humiliation of the previous October, the administration was in no mood to accommodate still another demonstration at the convention. In fact, they appeared to be moving in the other direction, toward rigidity and even repression. Shortly after the Pentagon confrontation, the government indicted the symbol of our "permissive" generation, Dr. Benjamin Spock, along with Yale chaplain William Sloan Coffin and others, on charges of conspiracy to promote draft resistance. Also indicted were the Oakland Seven, who led "Stop the Draft Week." And unknown to us, a "domestic war room" was created in the Pentagon, coordinating the efforts of 1,000 military intelligence agents gathering data and photographs on 18,000 citizens. Additionally, the FBI already had some 7,000 operatives at work on the perceived threat of the New Left, not to mention counterintelligence programs against the Panthers. Rennie and I met in New York with lawyers in late January to plan our effort to obtain Chicago permits for both a giant antiwar march and the Festival of Life visualized by members of the Youth International Party, the Yippies. We needed a group of legal volunteers on the streets in Chicago to obtain bail for those who would be arrested.

One of the law students who attended the meeting was Bernardine Dohrn, a bright, stunning, aggressive representative of the new forces flowing into SDS. Exhilarated by the Pentagon demonstration, she and other new SDS leaders had decided on a springtime offensive called "Ten Days That Shook the World," after John Reed's book on the Russian Revolution. The ambitious notion was that "actions" against the war and racism would take place on campuses across the country, attempting to resist and disrupt all ties to the military. After King's murder, the SDS chapter at Columbia University led a strike and occupied buildings, actions that were being repeated all across the country. I found myself on campus that week, chairing a meeting in the occupied Mathematics Building for an entire week before mass arrests were imposed. It did seem that something revolutionary was building, not only on American campuses but all across the world in that spring of 1968.

In this climate, Rennie and I were having a difficult time convincing SDS that our intended plans for Chicago should be supported. Rennie and I were becoming seen as old guard, or perhaps older sibling rivals of the new leadership, who classified us as politically "reformist," if not already "bourgeois."

It is true that we were not comfortable with the development of abstract rhetoric and fierce factionalism in the organization, which once had been like a family. Having abandoned Port Huron, the official SDS leaders now made such pronouncements as "To respect and operate within the realm of bourgeois civil liberties is to remain enslaved," or "The problem with participatory democracy is its basic inadequacy as a style of work for a serious radical organization." I was losing credibility with the organization, as was Rennie, although he remained far more in the pragmatic mainstream than I did.

We thought there still was a margin of opportunity for reforming America. Since late 1967, for example, Martin Luther King and SCLC had been trying to fashion a massive, nonviolent alternative to impending violent confrontations in black communities like Chicago's. While rejecting the use of rocks, bottles and guns from a moral and practical standpoint, King was struggling also to define another choice aside from the Black Power cry that was sweeping the ghettos. To save the worsening situation and prevent his personal irrelevance, King was talking of a "revolution of values," a "redistribution of power," and a last, desperate form of nonviolent civil disobedience. His idea, announced on December 4, 1967, drawn from the common experience of civil rights and ERAP projects, was for a Poor People's Campaign in the nation's capitol, starting in the late spring.

In the legal tyranny of the Deep South, marches had been forms of rebellion in themselves; but after his bitter Chicago experience of 1966, King felt that marches couldn't solve the crisis of the northern cities. King's plan, like that of the Bonus Marchers who brought their unemployment crisis to Washington in 1932, was to gradually besiege the nation's capital with an irresistible moral and political force of poor people: black, white, Latino and Native American. A mule train would lead a long march of the poor to Washington, where they would camp in parks and confront decision-makers with demands for ending their miseries. Among the most creative of the desperate protests suggested by King's aide Andrew Young was flooding Walter Reed Hospital, where elected officials were entitled to free health care, with hundreds of sick Americans demanding similar care for themselves.

Although King's advisers were as divided over the Poor People's Campaign as many antiwar activists were over our Chicago plans, Rennie and I both were excited about a potential meshing of the protests. The Kerner Report on Civil Disorders, commissioned by President Johnson immediately after Newark, had described the United States as "moving towards two societies, one black, one white—separate and unequal." The commission was recommending a thirty-billion-dollar program to create two million jobs, better schools, and more housing—exactly the annual cost of the Vietnam War. Perhaps we could work with Dr. King's campaign in the summer, with the mule train heading for Chicago at the time of the convention. Rennie called Abernathy and received an immediately favorable response. We were elated, for now it was all coming together.

TO: SAC [Special Agent in Charge], Albany   3/4/68
FROM: Director, FBI   PERSONAL ATTENTION

GOALS:

1. Prevent the coalition of black nationalist groups . . . An effective coalition of black nationalist groups might be the

first step toward a real "Mau Mau" in America, the beginning of a true black revolution.

2. Prevent the rise of a "messiah" who could unify, and electrify, the militant black nationalist movement. ████ * might have been such a messiah; he is the martyr of the movement today ... ████ could be a very real contender for this position should he abandon his "obedience" to "white, liberal doctrines" (nonviolence) and embrace black nationalism. ████ has the necessary charisma to be a real threat in this way.

3. Prevent violence on the part of black nationalist groups. ... Through counter-intelligence, it should be possible to pinpoint potential troublemakers and neutralize them before they exercise their potential for violence.

4. Prevent militant black nationalist groups and leaders from gaining respectability, by discrediting them ...

The next uplifting news item came from the McCarthy presidential effort. Fueled by post-Tet public discontent, 10,000 students were going door-to-door in the heavy snows. Before Tet, the president dominated McCarthy in national polls by 63 to 18 percent. In March, they were virtually even, and on primary day, March 12, McCarthy received a stunning 42.2 percent of the votes.

With some excitement now, Rennie and I put the finishing touches on an outline of our plans for Chicago, presenting it to a cross-section of about two hundred peace, civil rights, and radical activists who assembled outside of Chicago for the weekend of March 22–24. We were still facing an uphill effort in getting an endorsement for our project. We envisioned three days of decentralized protests across Chicago leading to a vast "funeral march" to the International Amphitheater on the last night of the convention, which we expected

* Material deleted by the FBI.

to end in Johnson's renomination. But because of our sympathies with the confrontation at the Pentagon, many traditional pacifists worried that we wanted to initiate violence. Our answer was that we *expected* violence, from the police and federal authorities, but we would not initiate it ourselves. Committing ourselves more formally to nonviolence, we wrote that while the demonstration would be "clogging the streets of Chicago with people demanding peace, justice and self-determination for all people," the protest campaign "should not plan violence and disruption against the Democratic National Convention. It should be nonviolent and legal."

This assurance, however, did not speak to the larger criticism hurled at the project from everyone suspicious of electoral politics. With McCarthy's upset showing in New Hampshire, it was widely assumed that any demonstrations in Chicago would turn into rallies for the Minnesota senator. Though Geoff Cowan, the planner of the challenge to the Humphrey delegates, was there to describe his "open convention" strategy, most of the people present were distinctly uninterested in electoral politics. They feared that instead of being on the cutting edge of change, the movement would be co-opted into liberal politics. Even worse, those in SDS and many others argued that lurking just behind Eugene McCarthy was the far more serious possibility of a Robert Kennedy candidacy. Wasn't the Chicago protest plan just a "stalking horse" for the Kennedy interests? They wanted to know. A widely quoted *Ramparts* article by Robert Scheer warned that Kennedy "could easily co-opt prevailing dissent without delivering to it . . . providing the illusion of dissent without its substance."

"Look," I argued, "whatever happens in the primaries, there will be a need for the peace movement to be at the convention to pressure the Democrats." I angrily announced at another point that we were not going to let this consultative meeting exercise a veto power over the idea of going to Chicago. Many people were enraged by this declaration. Staughton Lynd, who was now active in an ERAP-type project among industrial workers, thought I was risking the movement's

resources on a "one-shot" national fantasy. "You're leading this movement either into co-option by the Kennedy forces or into repression
and violence," another SDS leader charged. With that tone, the meeting ground to its inconclusive end.

FBI MEMORANDUM   **5/14/68**
FROM: Director
TO: SAC, Albany
**Counter Intelligence Program: Internal Security: Disruption
of the New Left.**

. . . <u>The purpose of this program is to expose, disrupt, and
otherwise neutralize the activities of the various new left
organizations, their leadership and their adherents.</u> It is
imperative that activities of those groups be followed on a
continuous basis so we may take advantage of all opportu-
nities for counterintelligence and also <u>inspire action where
circumstances warrant.</u> The devious maneuver, the duplic-
ity of these activists must be exposed to public scrutiny
through cooperation of reliable news media sources, both
locally and at the seat of government. <u>We must frustrate
every effort of these groups and individuals to consolidate
their forces or to recruit new or youthful adherents. In every
instance, consideration should be given to disrupting
organized activity of these groups and no opportunity
should be missed to capitalize on organizational or personal conflicts of their leadership.</u>
Offices which have investigative responsibility for <u>KEY
ACTIVISTS should specifically comment in the initial letter
to the bureau regarding these individuals.</u> These offices are

aware [that] these individuals have been identified as the moving forces behind the new left. No counter-intelligence action may be initiated by the field without specific bureau authorization.

The bureau has been very closely following the activities of the new left and the Key Activists and is highly concerned that the anarchistic activities of a few could paralyze institutions of learning, induction centers, cripple traffic, and tie the arms of law enforcement officials. All to the detriment of our society. The organizations and activists who spout revolution and unlawfully challenge society to obtain their demands must not only be contained, but must be neutralized. Law and order is mandatory for any civilized society to survive. Therefore, you must approach this new endeavor with a forward look, enthusiasm, and interest in order to accomplish our responsibilities. The importance of this new endeavor, cannot and will not be overlooked.

TO: SAC, Newark (100-48095)   5/17/68
FROM: Director, FBI (100-438281)
THOMAS EMMETT HAYDEN
SM-C
(KEY ACTIVIST)

Reference Buairtel [Bureau air telegram] captioned "Investigation of the New Left, Key Activists," dated 1/30/68.

. . . It will be incumbent upon the Bureau to intensify its investigations of those individuals who have assumed leadership in the new left. Hayden was designated a key activist in referenced Bureau airtel as a result of this leadership activity. Instructions as to the handling of this investigation were promulgated at that time.

It is to be noted that a recent edition of <u>Life</u> magazine carried a photograph of Hayden participating in the Columbia University demonstrations which effectively shut down that institution. No information in this regards was furnished by your office. This points out the apparent inadequacy of your day-to-day coverage. It should not be necessary for the Bureau to rely on news media for this type of information. Since Hayden has no connection whatever with Columbia University, it is obvious that what his expressed purpose for being on campus was to furnish leadership and assistance to the student revolt.

. . . The subject's travel both nationally and abroad should be closely followed. As office of origin, you will be expected to develop advance information in this regard and to issue sufficient instructions to offices in whose territory he is traveling to insure that his activities are fully covered while [he] is in a travel status. This phase of your investigation must be given close attention to insure that the Bureau is aware of his movements at all times.

No information is located in Bufiles [Bureau files] to indicate that you have conducted any investigation into Hayden's <u>financial activities</u>. You should promptly pursue this line of inquiry to develop his financial status, the source of his income, and the source of funds which enables him to travel. This should be a continuing project.

In evaluating this case, <u>you should bear in mind that one of your prime objectives should be to neutralize him in the new left movement. The Bureau will entertain recommendations of a counter-intelligence nature in order to accomplish this objective.</u> You should, therefore, furnish the Bureau with your suggestions along this line. Take no positive action however in this regard until you have received specific Bureau instructions.

The investigation of Hayden, as one of the key leaders of the new left movement, is of <u>prime importance</u> to the Bureau. You will be expected to pursue it <u>aggressively and with imagination</u>. Inadequate and delayed reporting of important developments will not be tolerated.

I had come to a simple, though high-risk, theory of ending the war. The Vietnamese would have to frustrate the U.S. military effort at a painful cost of lives on all sides; and the antiwar movement would have to impose a serious cost, a breakdown between the generations, on those intent on continuing the war. The resulting polarization would gradually bring a more rational alternative leadership into being on the national level. The antiwar movement would continue applying pressure, even on this more rational leadership, until the war ended. If that was not possible, I saw an unending spread of malignant strife. The "rational alternative" to the war and tumult, in the back of my mind, was Robert Kennedy. Otherwise there would be long-lasting polarization, perhaps civil war.

When Staughton Lynd and I met with Robert Kennedy in mid-February 1967, it was evident that he was rethinking his Vietnam policy, but still very cautiously. However, he was anti-LBJ, much closer to King than McCarthy could ever be, giving prescient environmental speeches, and sympathetic to the New Left's anti-poverty projects. Certainly it would be impossible for him to run for president without sharpening his opposition to Vietnam. Our movement could claim credit for building the climate of opinion that made an antiwar campaign possible. His success, however, would open the door to reform at just the moment blacks and young people were exploring more radical options. It was a dilemma we would have to accept as we proceeded.

The pace of history would not abate. As in a chapter from Mills's *Power Elite*, President Johnson summoned an advisory group, loosely known as the "wise men," to the White House. Most of them were members of the Council on Foreign Relations, major corporate attorneys who had served in high government positions over many years: Dean Acheson, George Ball, McGeorge Bundy, Arthur Dean, Douglas Dillon, Abe Fortas, Arthur Goldberg, Henry Cabot Lodge, John Jay McCloy, Robert Murphy, Cyrus Vance, and two generals, Omar Bradley and Matthew Ridgeway. The "wise men," at the direction of Secretary of Defense Clark Clifford, were asked to make a several-day private review of the Vietnam crisis and give the President their counsel. This they did and, according to the Pentagon Papers, convinced themselves that the U.S. policy had become completely counterproductive, that the war was a military failure, and that divisions in American society had become dangerously deep. Said Cyrus Vance, "We were weighing not only what was happening in Vietnam, but the social and political effects in the United States, the impact on the U.S. economy, the attitude of other nations. The divisiveness in the country was growing with such acuteness that it was threatening to tear the United States apart." Interestingly, they did not discuss the morality of the policies, only their overall cost-benefit ratios. On March 19, they had an elegant social luncheon with Lyndon Johnson, and when it was over, delivered their verdict: forget about seeking a battlefield solution to the problem and instead intensify efforts to seek a political solution at the negotiating table. The President was "greatly surprised at their conclusions."

Eleven days later, on Sunday, March 31, President Johnson went on television to offer a partial bombing halt over North Vietnam, appoint Averell Harriman to seek talks with the enemy, and withdraw himself from the 1968 presidential campaign.

I was sitting on a rug in a friend's living room in Newark. When Johnson read his withdrawal statement, I did a backward somersault from a sitting position.

On April 3, the first steps toward diplomatic talks between the United States and North Vietnam were announced. I sent a long telegram to Hanoi supporting their decision to come to the conference table and encouraging another release of POWs as a gesture of goodwill. (In February, Dave Dellinger and I had coordinated a second POW release, sending Father Daniel Berrigan and historian Howard Zinn to Hanoi to return with three U.S. pilots.) I made an appointment to see Harriman in Washington, as well as Sargent Shriver, the former Peace Corps director who had been appointed ambassador to France, where the talks would take place. The following day in Memphis, a 30.06 bullet killed Martin Luther King while he was preparing to go to dinner with friends during an intense period of demonstrations for the city's striking garbage collectors. I traveled early the next morning to Nashville, where I was to speak at Fisk University on a stage whose backdrop was a gigantic American flag. All I remember afterward was getting drunk with Julian Bond, an old friend from what now seemed to be a previous life. An Atlanta SNCC founder in 1960, Bond was now a Georgia state senator. We listened to the sirens and watched the military vehicles that patrolled angry Nashville. Stokely Carmichael, friends later told me, went berserk in those hours on the streets of Washington, waving a pistol and telling blacks to arm themselves. Bernardine Dohrn, weeping openly, joined other New York City activists in trashing store windows aimlessly in Times Square. I talked on the phone with Rennie in Chicago, where fires were being set across the city. Mayor Daley shortly issued an infamous order that his police officers should "shoot to kill" arsonists and "shoot to maim" looters.

Everything was without precedent as urban America blew up. There were outbreaks of black violence in over seventy-five cities and more than 70,000 troops were called in to reimpose order. Forty-six people were killed, nearly all of them black, 2,500 were injured, 28,000 were jailed, and fifty million dollars' worth of property damage occurred. In response to King's death, Congress finally passed a fair-housing law as a tribute. Attached to it was a little-noticed "anti-riot" amendment by Senator Strom Thurmond, making it a felony to travel between states with the "intent" of causing a "riot." The first and only persons to be indicted under this amendment would be the Chicago Eight.

I was torn apart with a grief which has not healed to this day. I went to Washington, while the city still burned, to keep my appointment with Harriman. Outside the windows of Harriman's office, one could see flames with smoke shooting up over the nation's capital and fire trucks and squad cars rushing everywhere. The secretaries were extremely tense, talking on the phones to their husbands and children about routes out of the city. Harriman, some seventy-seven years old, was about to leave for Paris, and the exploratory peace talks were on his mind. I briefed him as clearly as I could with the drama of urban rage flaring up behind his silver hair, describing my understanding of what the other side would be demanding at the talks, arguing that it was not yet too late for a political solution in South Vietnam, even with Johnson sitting as a lame-duck president. I also indicated that I would urge the North Vietnamese to release more American POW's. All I got from Harriman was a sense of optimism because talks were opening, as well as an interest in any possibilities of another prisoner release.

My time with Sargent Shriver was more productive, although rushed. He was leaving by limousine for his large home in the capital's suburbs and took me along so that we could discuss his Paris role. Sitting on the small seat across from him in the back of the limo, I was able to tell him in detail what Etienne Manac'h in the French foreign ministry had told me of the Vietnamese approach to settlement and give him the names of some French journalists and historians he might see privately in Paris. He seemed actively interested in playing whatever role he might while in Paris during the talks, I presumed as an intermediary for his brother-in-law, Robert Kennedy. I was pleased with his frankness, though I felt distinctly uncomfortable riding in a limousine while out the back window I could continue to watch the blaze above the skyline. "The last people who did this to us were the British," Shriver said with a laugh, referring to the city's burning during the War of 1812. When we finally reached his home, he thanked me and dispatched his driver to take me to the airport.

As I traveled through the country securing commitments from activists to come to Chicago, the question of the Democratic primary battle between McCarthy and Kennedy kept growing in importance. My close friend Jack Newfield was deeply involved with Kennedy, covering the campaign for the *Village Voice* and keeping notes for a book. Other friends, like Geoff Cowan, were now in charge of McCarthy's strategy of persuading delegates to support an "open convention." Yet in mid-May, a *Newsweek* poll gave Hubert Humphrey, who was campaigning only through proxies in the primaries while he lined up backroom Democratic support, a total of 1,279 delegates, to Kennedy's 713 and McCarthy's 280. It was becoming clear to me that if anyone could break open the tightly controlled convention, it was Kennedy with his greater ties to regular Democratic politicians, including Mayor Daley himself. The McCarthy camp remained bitterly opposed to Kennedy, however; sometimes, in fact, they seemed to prefer Humphrey to Kennedy.

As Kennedy explained to Newfield, and Newfield explained to me, a "new coalition" was needed for the Democratic Party and the country to hold together. Soured by organized labor's staunch support of Hubert Humphrey and the Vietnam War, Kennedy increasingly looked to racial minorities and the poor, along with students, as new forces that could be harnessed toward political change. But he could also reach the white ethnics, Newfield insisted. In short, Jack argued to me, Kennedy "agrees with you, but because of who he is, he can be elected president." Newfield showed me a napkin bearing Kennedy's scribbled signature. Late one night at a restaurant, the candidate had mischievously asked Jack what he wanted from an RFK presidency.

"Only two things," Jack immediately replied, "get out of Vietnam and make 'This Land Is Your Land' the national anthem." Kennedy, laughing, signed his agreement on the wrinkled napkin.

In San Francisco, I met with Kennedy adviser Richard Goodwin to explain the upcoming Chicago plans and ask the campaign's help in lobbying Mayor Daley for permits. Then I went to the Kennedy-McCarthy debate on June 1. It was held at the KGO television studios on Golden Gate Avenue.

Late that night, as I walked through the lobby of the Fairmont Hotel with Connie Brown, we came upon Robert Kennedy heading toward the elevator. He introduced me to astronaut John Glenn and others in his party, and we entered the elevator together. Though his expression had been fresh in the earlier debate, and his attitude clearly buoyant, he now appeared as tired as Newfield had described him. His eyes were withdrawn, his face lined and gaunt, his nose burned from the California sun. What struck me most, though, were his hands. Strong, athletic hands whose palms were nicked, scraped, and sore from thousands of outreaching hands of supporters in his motorcades. They reminded me of stigmata, of hands crucified.

"Are you helping? How's it look?" he asked quietly inside the elevator. "You won the debate tonight," I replied, "and I think it looks good. I want to work with your people on demonstrations in Chicago against the war."

"Good," was all he said, then his eyes drifted off to another thought. We reached his floor, and I shook the hand again. "Good luck," I said. "Thanks. Good night," he replied and patted his hand across Connie's back. The elevator door closed, and I watched him, almost limping down the hall, for the last time.

I saw the California election returns in a New York apartment with Len Weinglass, Connie, and several others. Newfield was on the fifth floor of the Ambassador Hotel in Los Angeles, and I expected to see him the following day. The next primary was in New York. If Kennedy won, Newfield said, it would possibly start an earthquake under the regular party delegates. If Kennedy lost California, on the other hand, Jack would title his book *The Late Senator Robert Kennedy.*

It was nearly 2:00 a.m. in New York when the returns showed Kennedy winning. I watched with a stirring of excitement as he introduced and thanked farm workers, along with black and labor activists who had labored to turn out their votes that day. He finished, exclaiming, "On to Chicago!"

In Los Angeles, Newfield and *Ramparts* editor Bob Scheer took the elevator down to the ballroom expecting to follow Kennedy to a party. Suddenly there came crackling, almost popping noises over the television, a cry in the confused crowd, a call for a doctor, and I knew it was over. On yet another haunted night, I stayed up watching the constant reruns: the words "On to Chicago," followed by the human wailing and the eerie kitchen scenes. I listened without hope to the periodic hospital reports, and without much credence to the early information on Kennedy's assassin. Sometime in the night, Jerry Rubin called in hysteria, saying he believed Sirhan did it "because he's an Arab." I called a few close friends as if I might never talk to them again. "I love you," I told one, thinking I might never have the chance to tell her. I was behaving, without quite recognizing it, as one does before one's own death.

The next day Newfield called. He caught the early-morning plane to escape Los Angeles and wanted to have dinner somewhere. Jack and his wife, *Voice* photographer Janie Eisenberg, showed up, stricken. Geoff Cowan and several other friends from McCarthy's campaign—Paul Gorman and Harold Ickes, Jr.—linked up with us somehow. In our emptiness, we decided to go to St. Patrick's Cathedral, where Bobby Kennedy's body awaited final ceremonies the next morning. When we arrived at the dark and massive cathedral, hundreds of New Yorkers were lining up outside. They were from various walks of life, but mainly they were poor and marginal people who had come to pay their respects as close to the funeral service as they could be. We walked through the silence to an entrance where we encountered a

Kennedy aide who invited us in. It must have been well after midnight, only a few hours before the opening of the cathedral for the service.

I sat down in a pew toward the back of the cavernous chamber. Police and carpenters were hard at work setting up wooden platforms for television crews. Priests hovered near the altar. Some Kennedy family and staff stood together trying to concentrate on arrangements. It was a while before I noticed the coffin of Bobby Kennedy. It was sitting by the altar rail, containing all that remained of last night's hopes of the poor. Nothing left of that hope now, gone in a coffin while crews hammered away and police awaited the crowd. I started to cry hard. After a while, the Kennedy aides motioned to me, asking that I come forward to the coffin. I walked slowly forward and, next to Geoff, stood in silent vigil. When morning came, I went home—"On to Chicago" repeating itself in my head.

Demonstration in Grant Park, Chicago, August 1968. PAUL SEQUEIRA

THE STREETS OF CHICAGO: 1968

The stunning events of the spring—LBJ's withdrawal, the Paris peace talks, the sudden deaths and the riots—left people depleted and plans for the convention protest in doubt. If the Paris talks signaled the beginning of peace, the war would no longer be a cause for marching; if the talks were a sham, what was the leverage on a president who already had withdrawn from the race? The big question was what could we hope to achieve with RFK dead and McCarthy no longer viable. What was the point?

I felt the plans for protest should go forward, if only to continue opposing a war which the president was trying to wipe off the front page during the election year. It appeared to me that the war was escalating in a new way. In late May, the American media reported the existence of a secret U.S. directive calling for an "all-out offensive against the enemy" over the summer. Though U.S. bombing had been halted in most of North Vietnam, bombing missions sharply increased over the "panhandle," the narrow strip of the North stretching down to the seventeenth parallel. The overall tonnage of bombs dropped on North Vietnam now was greater than before President Johnson's March 31 limitations. In July, the number of U.S. troops in South Vietnam increased by 19,000 to 535,000, and the *Times* reported that the "Pentagon's estimate of enemy troop strength has remained unchanged between 207,000 and 222,000 despite repeated charges of heavy enemy escalation." These reports increased my paranoia about what Johnson's "peace plan" actually meant.

Years later, I asked historian Doris Kearns about Lyndon Johnson's 1968 intentions. She was a White House intern in the 1960s, a dove, and a symbol to Johnson of the younger generation that he was losing. President Johnson became obsessed with Kearns, often arguing with her while also confessing his inner thinking. These conversations later became a book on the Johnson years, *Lyndon Johnson and the American Dream*, and made Kearns one of the few experts on the President's personal view of the times.

After Robert Kennedy's assassination, according to Kearns, Johnson briefly and ambivalently considered getting back into the presidential race. Stopping Robert Kennedy had been paramount for him. After RFK's death, he worried about a "draft Teddy" movement. "The way he would talk about it was by saying that all sorts of politicians were asking him to run, telling him that with the war on a better footing, he was the only one who could win," Kearns said. While these were largely fantasies, Johnson at least wanted to be present at the convention for his sixtieth birthday, on August 27. "He wanted them to fete his accomplishments and, if the convention fell apart, crazy as it seems, he would be there, available."

In retrospect, it is difficult to believe how closed the Democratic Party was. Of the 7.5 million Democrats who voted in the 1968 primaries, 80 percent voted for either Kennedy or McCarthy, and only 20 percent for Humphrey stand-ins. But the convention delegates already had been selected by Johnson's machine two years before. Therefore, reformers would be protesting inside a closed system. On the Chicago activist front, nothing was going very well either. SDS had moved unrecognizably to the left: Bernardine Dohrn was elected to the national leadership at their June convention, declaring, "I consider myself a revolutionary communist," which meant a supporter of the National Front for the Liberation of South Vietnam (NLF), the Cubans, and Third World revolutionaries in general. They continued to worry over the twin perils of repression and liberal reformism during Convention Week. The Yippies were having their troubles too; their local meetings and fundraising concerts were disrupted by Chicago police. Entertainers like Judy Collins began saying they could not perform in Chicago unless permits and sound systems were guaranteed. In New York, Jerry Rubin and Abbie Hoffman were privately debating a cancellation. The National Mobilization itself was internally divided and still had not issued an official call to Chicago by the summer, although Dave Dellinger was personally committed. In the official corridors of Washington and Chicago, there was hope that the protests could be squelched. In fact, a White House memo indicated that Democratic Party chairman John Bailey was "optimistic, and expects none of the major groups that originally planned demonstrations to go through with them," adding that "precautions will be taken [and] those attending the convention will leave Chicago remembering it as a friendly city." To discount such rumors, Rennie, Dave and I held unilateral press conferences on June 29 declaring that the demonstrations would happen—even though the cumbersome National "Mobe" still had not acted.

Rennie was getting nowhere in trying to meet with city officials about securing permits. Having negotiated with government officials for permits before, however, he was convinced that the city would wait until the last few days before the convention, in order to keep the numbers of protesters down, and then grant the permits.

According to one exhaustive history, the city decided as early as April not to issue permits or to cooperate in any way. The mayor's longtime press secretary said, "Our idea was to discourage the hippies from coming." The city was "not to give a staging ground" to the protestors by providing permits. Why should permits be given, he asked, for outside agitators "to plop on the ground" and "be taken care of?"

Unaware that such attitudes were already determined, Rennie tried a new approach, involving the U.S. Department of Justice. The department contained a little-known branch called the Community Relations

Service, headed by Roger Wilkins, Roy Wilkins's nephew and a talented negotiator whose assignments were usually to deal with mulish officials in southern cities. At Rennie's invitation, Wilkins flew to Chicago for a discussion of our plans and was asked to act as an intermediary with Mayor Daley. Rennie told me after the meeting how much he liked Wilkins, as I did when I met him later.

After meeting with Rennie, Wilkins sent a private memo to Attorney General Ramsey Clark that described Rennie as "an honest, intelligent man who was being candid with me" and recommended that

> the President and Vice President be apprised of the plans of the Mobilization, as we now know them, at the earliest possible time [and] one of them or someone clearly acting in their behalf call Mayor Daley to apprise him of that point of view and that the Mayor be advised that I will be coming to Chicago next week to inform him of the Mobilization's plans and . . . to set up a continuing working relationship between the city officials and the Mobilization.

Ramsey Clark, as far as I know, did not talk to Johnson or Humphrey, but refused FBI Director Hoover's request for wiretaps on several of us. It was arranged that in the following week Mayor Daley would talk with Roger Wilkins. But, according to Wilkins's account, the mayor was not interested in hearing our plans and seemed offended that federal officials would try to intervene in his city's affairs. Daley ended the meeting after about ten minutes.

Not long after, Wilkins again met with Rennie, this time bringing several Justice Department officials. One of them was Thomas Foran, a former political appointee of the mayor and the U.S. attorney for Chicago who would later be the chief prosecutor in the Chicago Eight trial. Hearing from Wilkins that Mayor Daley was opposed to any permits, Rennie made a direct appeal to Foran, the only official close to Daley, for help. Foran was noncommittal. But the very next day,

Deputy Mayor Stahl (whom we jokingly called "Stall") called the Mobe office. He complained about our going to the Justice Department but agreed to meet informally with Rennie. Rennie's stratagem had worked; we were ecstatic and believed the city would now be forced to grant us permits. It already was August 2, just over three weeks from the opening ceremonies of the convention. Time was of the essence.

Our hopes were quickly subdued. Meeting at a downtown coffee shop, Stahl told us that public parks couldn't be used as campsites, and the long-proposed march to the amphitheater was impossible for "security" reasons. In addition to these capricious views, Stahl's most telling comment, because of its clear dishonesty, was that all decisions regarding permits would be made by the Parks and Sanitation Department along with the police. In fact, as both sides at the coffee table knew, all such decisions in Chicago were made by one individual, Mayor Daley, not by lower bureaucrats. There was one last attempt at a City Hall meeting with Stahl, on August 12; it too ended in fiasco. On the same day, Senator McCarthy, after a personal appeal from Mayor Daley, made a public call for demonstrators to stay away from Chicago because of the "possibility of unintended violence or disorder." Shortly after, the open-convention advocates, including Allan Lowenstein and Geoff Cowan, were denied a permit for a Soldier Field rally and called off their activities for Convention Week.

On August 7, Vice President Humphrey's executive aide, William Connell, telephoned the FBI to ask for political intelligence on the upcoming Convention, as was provided President Johnson on the Mississippi Freedom Democrats in 1964. Hoover assistant Carla De Loach assured Connell that "the FBI's Chicago office is well prepared to gather intelligence and pass such intelligence on to appropriate authorities during the convention," and that "full preparations have been made by the Chicago Office to handle the matter of passing intelligence to the Vice President and his aides."

(In 2007, I interviewed Roger Wilkins, now a professor at George Mason University near Washington, D.C., asking him if the real conspiracy began with J. Edgar Hoover. Wilkins told me that while Hoover would not want to interfere with Daley, the FBI field agents would have been "infused with the Hoover worldview" including hatred of black revolutionaries and the New Left. But it went higher than Hoover, Wilkins told me. "As early as 1965, after Selma, the White House convened a cabinet-level task force under Hubert Humphrey. Humphrey started the meeting by saying 'You know, there is a lot of communist influence in Selma.' I was very upset with that view." Though becoming increasingly isolated from the White House, Wilkins continued working as an official mediator on Chicago through the Attorney General's office. "I liked Rennie, and the idea was to have Daley and the police commanders work out a modus vivendi, so if shit went down they would be able to communicate." When Wilkins met with Daley, "he couldn't get beyond my color. He thought I was warning him about blacks. He blamed everything on 'outside agitators' and actually said 'we know how to handle our [black] people, we put on carnivals.' The he got up from his desk, and the meeting was over." Wilkins subsequently wrote the Attorney General a memo saying mediation would fail and that "the events would be a national disaster and disgrace." Mayor Daley, he recalled, was "all over the place, besmirching me. He even blamed me later for Chicago.")

Our hopes not only for permits but for large numbers of demonstrators were beginning to collapse. How many people were going to spend four or five days in Chicago with no assurance that they could participate in a rally, attend a concert, march to the convention, or unroll a sleeping bag in Lincoln Park? Meeting continually now, some Mobe leaders—Dave Dellinger in particular—held out their belief that a lawsuit combined with public pressure would bring permits at the last hour, as happened the previous October on the eve of the Pentagon demonstration.

My mood darkened. "They're just fucking around with us, stalling for time, and they have no intention of giving us permits," I argued in a late-night meeting. They want to keep most people out of town and drive the rest of us off the streets. We can't back down. We're not just protesting the war. We have to fight for the streets. We have to fight just for our right to be here." The city's strategy was working effectively to reduce our numbers, but it would backfire, I thought, in another way, by building an American iron curtain around the convention and creating a police state in the streets.

I went out later for a beer with John Froines. John and his wife Ann had been through ERAP with me, and we shared a passion about Vietnam. Like many people, John wanted to devote himself to an academic career but felt pulled into the vortex of Chicago. John recalls my saying that night that twenty or twenty-five people could die in the convention protests. If I did, I have blanked it out, but I do remember thinking that it was time to prepare for the worst scenario. The experimental questioning of American society that began at Port Huron was yielding bitter evidence; America was turning out to be more like Mississippi than not. How much difference was there, after all, between Jackson, Mississippi, and Mayor Daley's Chicago? In the South, we could at least appeal to a higher, and arguably more tolerant, level of government; in this case, that higher level in Washington was fully aligned with Chicago's City Hall. At Port Huron, we believed that apathetic individuals could be transformed into active, thinking citizens who could influence government by building local organizations. Here in Chicago, every organization we had tried to build—the JOIN Community Union, the April 27 Peace Coalition, and many others— had been routinely harassed, raided, sprayed with Mace, attacked by police and denied even the smallest victories of the kind we were able to achieve in Newark. There was the shoot-to-kill, shoot-to-maim rhetoric. And now, by denying permits, Mayor Daley—and the White House behind him—was smugly denying that the First Amendment should protect the rights of hippies to sleep in a park, or McCarthy workers to rally at Soldier Field, or the Mobilization to assemble at the amphitheater. I was convinced we had to lay aside whatever hopes we harbored for respectability, for career, for step-by-step reform. It was a time to risk our necks to take democracy back, a time no longer for visionary platforms but for suffering and physical courage. I told a New York audience that they should come to Chicago prepared to shed their blood.

Albert Camus had warned against the politics of resentment I was beginning to embody, calling it an "evil secretion, in a sealed vessel of prolonged impotence." But I believed that I was still acting in the spirit of Camus' rebel, and partly I was. His rebel was never realistic, nor was I then. Rebellion, for Camus, was "apparently negative, since it creates nothing," but it turned out to be "profoundly positive, in that it reveals the part of man which must always be defended." We had to resist police and political oppression in Chicago, I felt, not because it was realistic but because not acting meant succumbing.

The protest plan for the convention, now only twelve days away, was being refashioned constantly. We repeatedly tried to explain its outline to city officials:

August 24: A decentralized "people's assembly" at over a score of "movement centers," where individuals would receive a briefing about the week's schedule, and meet for the first time;

August 25: Opening day of the convention: nonviolent and legal picketing on sidewalks outside delegates' hotels in the Loop;

August 26: Rallies and meetings in Lincoln, Grant and Hyde Parks;

August 27: Concert and rally at Coliseum, Yippie Festival;

August 28: Day of Humphrey's nomination: rally in Grant Park, march ten miles to International Amphitheater;

August 29: Decentralized actions at institutions representing war and racism.

If the city gave us a last-minute permit, so much the better. If not, we would have to become very creative. One of the key factors in our survival now was the training of about one hundred Mobilization marshals who, in a situation without rules, would have to play an important leadership role on the streets. In past demonstrations, marshals were used mostly as traffic directors, guiding people toward a rally site, keeping marchers in orderly lines, shouting instructions or chants over bullhorns. But Chicago had to be approached differently. Instead of a "vertical" organization with leaders in front and followers marching obediently behind, we would need a "horizontal" structure of small groups as the vital base of the Mobilization. There was too clearly a danger that leaders like ourselves would be arrested or hurt, cut off from the mass of activists. Further, as we wrote in the instructions to the marshals, the police were expected to "operate from a strategy of containment and mass arrest rather than indiscriminate brutality." This meant a danger of hundreds or thousands of people being encircled and removed from the streets before the convention came to its climax on August 28. We wanted to fill the streets as much as possible, not be held in jails on exorbitant bail.

Therefore, it was necessary to improvise what we called "mobile tactics." During parts of Convention Week, small groups of fifty to one hundred demonstrators would picket at a decentralized site, for example, a draft board office. That way, if they were rounded up, thousands of others would remain at large. On the other hand, for situations when large assemblies would come together, the marshals were being trained to lead people out of the danger of mass arrest. The marshals awkwardly tried to mimic the "snake dances" used by Japanese students as a way to break out of police lines while avoiding either attacks by demonstrators on police or leaving isolated individuals behind. A few practiced karate self-defense moves, teaching techniques for protecting vital organs from police clubs and boots. But it was amateur theater compared to the riot-control techniques that were efficiently being practiced by the National Guard against simulated long-haired demonstrators during the summer. In response we trained our marshals in makeshift first-aid techniques against head wounds, serious bleeding, and tear-gas or Mace attacks. Marshals also studied by map and on foot most of the throughways, bridges, and alleys from Lincoln Park to Grant Park and to the amphitheater.

On August 22 in Lincoln Park, the police shot and killed Jerome Johnson, a 17-year-old Indian teenager. Johnson, an early arrival for the Festival of Life, was said to have "threatened" the officers who killed him. The next day, Judge Lynch (another aptly named friend of the mayor's) rejected our appeal for permits; the National Guard was provided fifteen sites for sleeping and assembling. There was nothing further to negotiate. The sides were now assembled, as in a medieval battle.

In their camp were 11,000 Chicago police on full alert; 6,000 National Guardsmen with M-I rifles, shotguns, and gas canisters; 7,500 U.S. Army troops; 1,000 federal agents from the FBI, CIA, and army and navy intelligence services (one of every six demonstrators was an undercover agent, they would claim later). Electronic surveillance was conducted against the Mobilization, the Yippies, McCarthy headquarters, and the broadcast media. The amphitheater was secured with a 2,000-foot barbed-wire fence, roadblocks in every direction, a ban on low-flying aircraft, and electronic equipment to certify the identity of delegates. The convention police command was centralized in a secure headquarters at the amphitheater, complete with giant electronic maps of Chicago, video and radio links to every security unit, and hotlines to the White House and Pentagon.

On our side were approximately 1,000 people, mainly in their early twenties, waiting nervously in a park, looking for places to sleep.

It was Saturday morning, August 24, one day before the official opening of the convention. I was sleeping late. The bedroom door opened. Drowsily, I saw a naked woman who had risen earlier. Maybe she'll come back to bed, I was thinking, when she said quietly:

"There's a man outside with a gun."

Well. No need for coffee then. She went back to observe him through the front-room curtains while I dressed and composed a plan. Grabbing an apple, I jumped out the kitchen window of the apartment building in Hyde Park, ran several blocks, and hopped the El train to Chicago's Loop. There I made my way through thick crowds of shoppers to our Mobilization offices, high in an office building on South Dearborn.

When I left the elevator at the floor of our office, there was a beefy, casually dressed man with crossed arms, menacing eyes, and greased hair standing against the wall. A hit man, I thought, and quickly entered the office. Rennie was there already and asked, smiling, "Have you met yours yet?" He had first encountered the man now outside the office door on his apartment steps that morning.

Our two plainclothes tails were Chicago police officers named Ralph Bell and Frank Riggio, although they never introduced themselves formally. They were assigned to follow us wherever we went at the fairly claustrophobic distance of about ten feet. We went to the bathroom; they followed. We went to lunch; they sat glowering at the next table. We drove to a meeting; they lurched behind in their car. When close enough, they made remarks about "getting" us, or "arresting you every time you're in the streets." The larger of them, Bell, had a real habit of losing his temper, getting wild-eyed, moving close, and threatening to do away with me on the spot. A phone call notified us that Jerry and Abbie were being followed too.

If this is a preview, I thought, we are not going to be free to meet or plan, and we will be lucky to survive. The week's events were grim already; now we were being followed by characters usually found in cheap movies about the Soviet Union.

By the afternoon, more and more demonstrators were arriving, filling Lincoln Park, getting to know each other, looking over maps of the city, taking down phone numbers for legal aid, mainly waiting apprehensively for some direction. As night fell, the Yippies, who had nominated a live pig for president the day before on a platform of "garbage," were urging compliance with the 11:00 p.m. curfew. Allen Ginsberg, chanting *om*, believed he could calm the tension with the police. At 11:00 p.m. promptly, the police surged through the park on motorcycle and foot, removing a few hundred people but with minimal arrests.

As the delegates arrived in their hotels the following day, August 25, we felt that the curtain of uncertainty caused by the lack of permits had to be pulled back and tested in daylight. With Rennie carrying a bullhorn and taking the lead, we marched from Lincoln Park all the way to the Loop's hotels—without incident. However, uniformed and plainclothes officers, including Bell and Riggio, strode beside us all the way, quarreling over the details of the route, until we reached Grant Park, across from the Conrad Hilton Hotel, where we dispersed. We were pleased, but no more certain of where the police would draw the line.

Lincoln Park was absolutely eerie, filled with the silhouettes of young dropouts, militant protestors, McCarthy volunteers, voyeurs, and undercover agents. This would be the night, I sensed, that the battle for Lincoln Park could get out of hand. The convention was beginning the next morning, most of the protesters had arrived, and the police would try to establish dominance. An anticipation of police harassment held the people together, allowing them to forget the relatively low turnout of 1,000 or more. If the police had done nothing, the protest might have fizzled, directionless. But it wasn't to be.

Off and on during the preceding two days I had lost my police tails, only to have them show up at the next place or event where they expected me. On Sunday night they found me in the park and began glaring from behind trees as I wandered through the crowd. If there was going to be a confrontation at 11:00 p.m., I knew that Rennie and

I would not survive it one minute if we were closely tailed. I also knew that I would get little sleep unless I could get away from these pursuers to a safe and quiet apartment for the rest of the night.

A plan took shape. Bell and Riggio had driven their unmarked car into the park before following us on foot. If a tire was deflated, they could be stopped cold. With mingled friends providing protection, I stepped out of sight, circled the park, and approached the darkened car. An accomplice named Wolfe Lowenthal took most of the air out of one tire when Bell and Riggio suddenly appeared out of the trees, saw Wolfe at work, and quickly grabbed him. I ran up, and they turned on me, holding me against the vehicle, trying to shove me inside. What saved me from taking a very rough ride in that unmarked car was a crowd that quickly gathered around the officers, chanting, "Let him go, let him go!" Bell and Riggio, sensing their loss of control, backed away. When I last looked back, they were stooped over, fixing their rear tire.

The police waited until an hour past eleven to enforce the curfew that night, then swept Lincoln Park with clouds of tear gas. Our preparations for the gas attack were minor; people were instructed to cover their faces with Vaseline and soaking handkerchiefs or towels, even the sleeves of their shirts if necessary. But the gas canisters did their job, turning the balmy night air into a jolting, choking, inescapable darkness. It was as if someone held me down and stuffed pepper in my mouth, nose, and eyes. The impact made everyone gradually give way, screaming at the police or throwing rocks at their shotguns, then running blindly in whatever direction promised relief from the clouds of gas. The streets around the park were jammed for hours, as the citizens of Chicago began to feel the presence of confrontation for the first time. Some motorists shouted their sympathy, but most were enraged at the tie-up or immobilized at the sight of police weaving on foot between cars, clubbing people into the pavements. The police also unleashed a volley of hate toward the press, beating many reporters and photographers who were wearing their press badges and attempting to cover the melee.

Temporarily free of Bell and Riggio, I slept a few hours on the couch of Vivian and Richie Rothstein's apartment. The next day, Monday, August 26, the convention formally began. McCarthy supporters and dissident Democrats now held out no hope for derailing Humphrey, who, in addition to restating his allegiance to Johnson's policies, was making obsequious statements of support for the Chicago police. The only hope remaining to the progressive delegates calling for an open convention was a Vietnam peace plank they sought to add to the Democratic platform. The platform committee's draft endorsed Johnson's policies, however, despite the fact that a 53 percent majority of Americans in the Gallup poll now thought the war was a "mistake," up from 25 percent two years before. The alternative peace plank, calling for cessation of the bombing of North Vietnam, a mutual troop withdrawal from South Vietnam, and a coalition government in Saigon, would have a lot of delegate appeal, I thought. It would also bring Lyndon Johnson all the way from the Pedernales River, if necessary, to crush it. "He called me at the convention, where I was with my antiwar friends," Doris Kearns remembered. "He wanted to come, was planning to come. He went on for fifteen minutes about how the country was rejecting him."

I went to Lincoln Park for a meeting of our marshals early that afternoon. Since it appeared that the police would continue to gas, club, and arrest people to drive us away from the convention areas, we needed an emergency response plan. Our exhausted medical volunteers were working on the injured and supplying crucial advice on coping with tear gas. How could we keep the police from arresting them? Our legal teams were similarly swamped, between bailing people out of jail all night and taking down endless affidavits against police brutality. They were frustrated on many levels, for example, by the police practice of covering their identifying badges with tape before the clubbing began. Virtually all communication with city officials, police commanders, and Justice Department liaisons was over. As we contemplated what to do, I noticed a police wagon and a second vehicle bouncing straight over the grass, coming our way, pulling to a stop less than a hundred feet from us. After a moment, Bell and Riggio, backed by several uniformed and club-wielding officers, jumped out. There was no escape, so I simply said to the marshals, "I'm going to be arrested right now." The officers grabbed me by the arms and marched me into the wagon along with Wolfe Lowenthal, and we took off on a bumpy and rapid ride downtown while a surprised and angry crowd gathered in our way on the grass.

"I oughta kill you right now," Riggio said as we rode in the cramped back compartment of the van. He was nervously dragging on a cigarette and staring at me as if I were an animal. I concentrated on what to do if he started carrying out his threat. "But you're gonna get it. You're gonna get federal charges and go away for a long time." There it is, I thought. He's already been given the big picture by someone. And this is only day one of Convention Week. They jailed me downtown. Several floors below me I could hear marchers shouting, "Free Hayden!" Another demonstration had been permitted, I thought happily. The rules were changing by the moment. I rested quietly in my cell, trying to plan how I was going to make it through this week on the streets outside. My thinking was interrupted by a jailer who unlocked the cell door, informing me that I was bailed out.

Relieved that it was not yet dark, I quickly left the station—only to discover a new man with a gun, leaning against the wall of the precinct. As I groaned to myself, he said, "Well, I've finally caught up with you." He was the original tail, who had waited outside my apartment Saturday morning. He sauntered close behind me as I looked for Rennie to get a report on the day's events and the night's expected chaos. We reconnected, were surprisingly able to lose my newest tail in the Chicago traffic, and decided to cruise by Lincoln Park as curfew neared.

FBI MEMORANDUM   **9/20/68**

████ * advised that he was one of the officers assigned to a surveillance team on Thomas Hayden during the daytime hours. During that four day period, ████ and his partner, ████ spent most of their time trying to locate Hayden, who actively made every effort to lose his police escort through that period. Due to the crowds, Convention, and demonstration-type activities, Hayden was successful in these efforts.

The second night was worse than the first. In addition to the heavy gas, the police fired salvos of blanks from shotguns at the crowd in Lincoln Park. Allen Ginsberg and his friends seemed to think they could blissfully vibrate the violence away, and I'm sure he was disappointed that so many of us were consumed with what he considered negative energy. At the time I thought, however, that Ginsberg was crazy, sitting cross-legged in the grass, eyes closed, chanting *om* over and over while the police lines tightened. The scene was totally surreal; a cultural war between thousands of police and protesters just blocks, even doors, away from the exclusive Gold Coast section of Chicago, where the affluent citizens went about their "normal" lives, trusting the police to keep their existence sanitized. It was crazier still in the Loop, where convention delegates wearing straw Humphrey hats, festooned with candidate buttons, were partying in the lounges just a sidewalk away from the police lines and the ominous darkness of Grant Park.

I was watching the delegates return from the amphitheater to the Conrad Hilton about midnight, when I encountered Jack Newfield, Geoff Cowan, and Paul Gorman, the McCarthy speech writer. They described how Hubert Humphrey that night had cemented his pact with the southern Democrats against the antiwar liberals in pushing

---

* Material deleted by the FBI.

for the status-quo platform plank on Vietnam. I tried to explain how insane it was in the streets, but it was as if we were in two worlds, invisible to each other. They invited me into the Hilton, where they had rooms. I got as far as the revolving door, where a hotel officer held out his arm. "We don't want this man in here," he said. Bemused, my friends started arguing that I was their guest. I became jittery. Just across Michigan Avenue a line of police was confronting a new crowd of demonstrators. Suddenly, Riggio appeared at the edge of our circle, smoking a cigarette, staring at me, his boots pawing the ground. "Forget it," I said and started to cross the street, careful to move away from the confrontation brewing in the park.

Suddenly, I felt the hint of a tornado over my right shoulder. Out of nowhere came Bell, charging like a linebacker, crashing both of us to the street, beating my head, dragging me through the kicking boots of other police, twisting my arm in a karate hold, and slamming me into a police car. It was just after midnight, and I was going back to jail for a second time.

The atmosphere in the detention room was ugly. I noticed among the thirty or so prisoners the faces of many younger SDS members— Bill Ayers of Ann Arbor, Terry Robbins of Cleveland, Jeff Jones from the Columbia strike—who had worked in civil rights and community projects. Whereas my first taste of violence in the South allowed me to *hope* for a response from the national government, their introduction to mindless sadism was coming at the convention of the Democratic Party and Johnson administration. In two years, several of them would decide to form the Weather Underground and engage in an offensive of guerrilla violence. Tonight they were sprawled on the floor, nursing cuts and bruises, listening to raging officers call them scum and threaten to beat them to death. Fortunately, Newfield, Geoff's brother, Paul Cowan, and Jim Ridgeway—all writers for the *Village Voice*—followed me to police headquarters and, after two hours, bailed me out. When I left the jail, it was three or four in the morning, and with my friends I walked the streets trying to get my bearings.

It was no time to be arrested again, and I wondered where I could be safe. As Newfield later recalled that night, "Almost every noise was martial: fire sirens, the squawking of two-way radios, cop cars racing from place to place, the idle chatter of police on duty." I felt naked. I could not be me, not on the streets of Chicago.

As we wandered down the street, several prostitutes approached us, asking if we wanted sex. They were black, well dressed, and wore pink sunglasses and large McCarthy-for-President buttons. "No thanks," I said politely. "I just got out of jail."

"You did?" the lady replied. "So did we."

I grabbed a taxi to the *Ramparts* magazine office, where they published a daily "wall poster" on the convention. They would be up all night, and I could find sanctuary, coffee, a couch, and contemplate a solution to my problem.

Late the next afternoon, Tuesday, August 27, a new Tom Hayden appeared on the streets. Behind the fake beard, sunglasses, neck beads, and yellow-brimmed hat which I alternated with a football helmet, no one knew me. A friend procured a variety of disguise materials and by dusk I was ready to rejoin people in the streets. My friends didn't know me until they heard my voice. To others, I looked like an undercover cop or random weirdo. I strolled right by the police. Bell and Riggio were hopelessly lost.

That night, the "Unbirthday Party" for President Johnson was held in the coliseum, a peaceful sanctuary for bringing together the whole coalition. There were bruised faces and bandaged heads, diehard McCarthy volunteers, the tattered and tired and tenacious listening to Phil Ochs singing "I Ain't Marching Anymore" and "The War Is Over." At the chorus, somebody lit and raised a match in the darkened theater. Somebody else. And another. Ten. Fifty. Five hundred. A candlelight chorus, everyone singing, crying, standing, raising fists, reaching delirium at the words, "Even treason might be worth a try / The country is too young to die."

The reformist spirit of the civil rights movement, withered and repressed, had turned into the militant rhetoric of the Black Panther Party, whose chairman, Bobby Seale, flew in from Oakland to address the crowd in Lincoln Park the next day, Wednesday. The Panthers were the living incarnation of Frantz Fanon's "revolutionary native" for whom the acceptance of violence was a purifying step toward self-respect. Formed in late 1966, they carried out the call of Malcolm X for armed self-defense. Like Malcolm, they were street people, "brothers off the block," channeling the chaotic rage into armed street patrols, a newspaper that reached 200,000 people weekly, a children's breakfast program, and a support network that enjoyed massive backing in black communities, especially among young people. Their founder, Huey P. Newton, was a mythic figure on the streets of Oakland; he was imprisoned for a gun battle in late October 1967 that left one Oakland policeman dead, another seriously wounded, and Huey shot in the stomach. Yet, because of the Panther presence, Oakland was one of the few black ghettos that never erupted in spontaneous violence in the late 1960s. Even two days after the murder of Martin Luther King, when a Panther named "L'il Bobby" Hutton was shot and killed while surrendering to Oakland police along with Eldridge Cleaver, the community remained still. Because of this focus on an almost military discipline, the Panthers initially considered the Yippies foolish anarchists and urged their members to stay away from Chicago during the convention. But under the lyrical spell of Eldridge Cleaver, a convicted rapist whose *Soul on Ice* was a nationwide bestseller, the Panthers began to reconsider their stand on Chicago, embracing the notion that a cultural rebelliousness among young white people was a necessary prelude to their becoming real revolutionaries.

Seale flew in to endorse the Chicago demonstrations in the middle of the week. While only there a few hours, he gave a speech having

Bobby Seale speaking at a rally in Chicago, spring 1969.
NACIO JAN BROWN

nothing to do with Chicago but rich enough in violent metaphors to lead to his indictment a year later, reflecting the Panthers' militant rhetoric of the time A tape recording of his speech in Lincoln Park was later played during the trial:

> Is the white racist wall that we're talking about real or not? . . . You're damned right it's real. Because we're chained against this wall.
>
> . . . Don't be out there jiving, wondering whether the wall is real or not. Make sure if you want to coalesce, work, functionally organize, that you pick up a crowbar. Pick up a piece. Pick up a gun . . .
>
> Now, there are many kinds of guns. Many, many kinds of guns. But the strongest weapon that we have, the strongest weapon that we all each individually have, is all of us. United in opposition. United with revolutionary principles.
>
> . . . On the streets, stop running in large groups. That ain't no right tactic. We should run in groups of fours and fives—all around. We cannot continue using these tactics where we lose 3,000 arrested or we lose one or two hundred dead. We gotta stop. So we want to start running in threes, fours, and fives. Small groups using proper revolutionary tactics. So we can dissemble those pigs who occupy our community, who occupy our community like foreign troops.
>
> We hope, we sure that you can begin to set up a few things organizationally to deal with the situation in a very revolutionary manner. So, Power to the People. Power to All the People. Black Power to Black People. Panther Power. Even some Peace and Freedom Power.*

It must have been a truly disorienting sight for the undercover agents: a stern Black Panther in beret and black leather jacket boasting

---

* A complete transcript of Bobby Seale's speech as introduced in the trial can be found here: http://www.law.umkc.edu/faculty/projects/ftrials/Chicago7/Seale.html.

of the necessity of "picking up the gun," together with a hairy Yippie dressed, I recall, in love beads and a plastic bandolier. It is a measure of the alienation of the times that what seem now to be caricatures of rebellion could have been taken seriously, but they were. The black underclass was connecting with overprivileged whites in a strange and explosive alliance of resentment and guilt. It was deadly serious, especially to Rubin's personal bodyguard, one of several undercover agents posing as Panthers and Yippies in the crowd.

Though nothing happened after Seale's appearance, it was only a matter of several hours before the nightly ritual of battle resumed. This time a group of ministers held a vigil around a large wooden cross they carried into Lincoln Park. Over 1,000 people sang the "Battle Hymn of the Republic," "Onward, Christian Soldiers," and "America the Beautiful" before a huge city truck began gassing them more heavily than the previous night. In addition, our medical stations were overrun and smashed, and numerous reporters were again beaten badly. Again, the nearby streets were choked with running figures, with rocks, bottles, and police batons everywhere in the air. From Lincoln Park, we began trotting in twos and threes southward, over the several bridges on the way to the Loop and Grant Park, where the delegates were returning from the convention. I remember running the several miles, fearing that the police would order the drawbridges lifted to cut us off.

Once outside the Hilton Hotel, we took a dual approach to the returning Democratic delegates. For the most part, we tried chanting "Join us! Join us!" A number of them actually did, especially as the week went on. But for the LBJ-Humphrey delegates, drinking nightly in the bars, filled with alcoholic disgust for hippies, we had another approach. They became the targets of our secret guerrilla-theater unit, a small group with the goal of exposing, surprising, and confronting delegates with the need to take sides. Mainly women, they dressed smartly and strolled through security lines without incident. Kathy Boudin and Cathy Wilkerson used lipstick to scrawl VIETNAMESE

ARE DYING on the mirrors in ladies' rooms, and spray painted "CIA" in huge red letters outside an office we believed to be the agency's local headquarters. Connie Brown and Corrina Fales, along with Kathy, dropped stink bombs in the Go-Go Lounge of the Palmer House, by dipping facial tissues into butyric acid, a chemical that smelled like rotten eggs. Connie was caught red-handed by a security guard. "I don't know what you're talking about," she protested to the guard. But she couldn't explain the foul-smelling odor coming from her purse. She was hustled away; feeling sorry for her, Corrina and Kathy turned themselves in as well. The three were thrown into cells filled with black lesbians and told by furious Chicago police that they would be jailed for twenty years. Kathy was particularly worried because she was planning to enter law school. Months later, on the advice of her father—noted attorney Leonard Boudin—the three pled guilty to malicious destruction of property and served no time. They became "unindicted co-conspirators" in the Chicago conspiracy trial one year later. Kathy never attended law school; two years later she joined the Weather Underground, and in 1984 she pleaded guilty to second-degree murder and armed robbery and was sentenced to twenty years to life.

There were far worse ideas circulating spontaneously. For a friend of mine from the New York Motherfuckers who threw a sharp-edged ashtray at the faces of the police, yelling, "Here goes a provocateur action," this was the apocalypse. Another proclaimed to anyone listening, "You're not a free person until the pig has taken your honkie blood!" At one point I even prepared a tape to be played and amplified from inside the Hilton to embarrass the police into thinking I had penetrated their thick lines. The tape ended by calling on the protestors to "join me." Wiser and more cautious heads decided to throw the tape away before anyone tried to follow me. It was difficult not to be immersed in a frenzy. Jack Newfield, who was worried about my militancy, later admitted that he had thrown a typewriter from a Hilton window at the police below.

About 2:00 a.m., the police commander curiously announced on a bullhorn that we could stay in Grant Park overnight, provided we were peaceful. A triumphant cheer of relief went up, and the tension was transformed into a more idyllic collective experience. People were lying on the comfortable grass, singing protest songs with Peter, Paul, and Mary with the floodlit Hilton in the background. At moments like these, it was perfectly clear how peacefully the protests of Convention Week might have gone.

At 3:00 a.m., the reason for the relaxed police behavior became stunningly apparent as the first units of the National Guard began advancing down Michigan Avenue. Not only did they bear M-1 rifles, mounted machine guns, and gas masks, but they were accompanied by vehicles we'd never seen before, jeeps with giant screens of barbed wire attached to their front bumpers, which we came to call "Daley dozers." They abruptly took positions in front of us, menacing but making no move. A few protestors starting shouting, "Chicago is Prague!"

While the extreme tension continued, many of our people could take it no more and began lying down on the grass or in sleeping bags to rest before the sun came up. I became worried, as did our marshals, that a preemptive mass street arrest might be launched by the Guard, sweeping us off these streets as the very day of Humphrey's nomination dawned. I took a bullhorn and told everybody to go home. Then I left quickly to get a few hours' sleep myself before the most critical day of the convention.

That night the police carried their vendetta against the media onto the convention floor, where a security officer slugged Dan Rather. On national television, Rather said, "This is the kind of thing going on outside the hall. This is the first time we've had it happen inside the hall. I'm sorry to be out of breath, but somebody belted me in the stomach." Walter Cronkite added, "I think we've got a bunch of thugs here, Dan."

I was exhausted. I asked Bob Ross, who also lived in the Kimbark building, if he would stay with me in the streets the next night. After being arrested and hunted, I told him that I was worried about what the police might do if they caught me again.

FBI MEMORANDUM 9/20/68

■■■■■* learned from other individuals, primarily Rubin and his fellow Yippie Abbie Hoffman, that Hayden had been an active participant in the street disturbances . . . Rubin and Hoffman together with assorted associates were in the habit of discussing events of the previous evening over their morning meals, and it was during these conversations that remarks were made indicative of the fact that Hayden had been one of the few demonstration leaders who actually had taken part in the street action on the occasions previously referred to . . .

■■■■■* volunteered the opinion, based on ■■■■■* and his observations of Hayden, that Hayden was one of the most likely among their number to deliberately start or create an incident of violence, since Hayden appeared to be one of the few in this leadership who does not mind, or fear, actual participation in disorder . . . it was extremely difficult to remember specific or isolated remarks and incidents . . . Hayden made remarks at various times to the effect that the strength and future of the movement lay in the young people in this country who must be induced to follow the lead of himself and his associates. There was no question that their goal is generally the radical remaking of the structure and form of the United States Government, including its overthrow if necessary.

* Material deleted by the FBI.

With little or no rest, our leadership met the next morning—Wednesday, August 28, the day of Hubert Humphrey's ascension to the presidential nomination and the day long anticipated as the showdown between the protestors and official powers.

Dave, Rennie, and I led a meeting in the empty, gray, paper-littered Mobe office. John Froines attended, as did Irv Bock, an undercover agent from the Chicago Police Department posing as the representative of the Chicago Peace Council. Irv was one of the week's marshals, a big, strong fellow who claimed to have time off from his job with American Airlines. He was suspicious since he didn't fit the stereotype of a protester, but at this point his presence didn't bother us; we had nothing to hide now. Though weary and strained, we had to decide the most crucial questions of the week. Even if the demonstrations were mainly spontaneous, we had the heavy duty of calling the actions, setting the time and place, communicating with the police and press, and making sure that medical and legal help was available.

The dilemmas before us that morning arose from the physical impossibility of achieving our longstanding goal of reaching the amphitheater, about ten miles south of the Loop, at the moment of Humphrey's nomination. We were bottled up in the parks, yet we could not stand by in silence. We did not relish more violence, certainly not after the previous night, but we did want direct moral engagement with the delegates and politicians who we felt were selling out the country.

What, we asked ourselves, were our options? The police were offering the Grant Park Bandshell, near Lake Michigan, about a half mile from the Hilton, for a strictly contrived afternoon rally where we would be allowed to voice our grievances, then be ordered to disperse. This was completely unacceptable from our standpoint. The police wanted our rally to end in the afternoon, while we wanted to demonstrate *during* the nomination proceedings at night. And I suspected that the police were planning to surround us at the bandshell to prevent another night of protest in Grant Park across from the Hilton—the closest thing to demonstrating at the convention site.

We agreed that there should be a rally at the bandshell at noon, to take advantage of the temporary police permit and try to involve those thousands of Chicago citizens who were simply afraid to join us at night. We agreed on music, poetry, and speeches by a cross section of movement leaders and victims of violence. But there were only two choices for those who intended to remain after the "legal" rally. The first, preferred by Dave, was to organize a nonviolent march toward the faraway Amphitheater. This, of course, would be blocked promptly by the police and probably end in mass arrests without even getting out of the bandshell area. The second notion was to get out of the park by mobile tactics after the rally and regroup in front of the Hilton by the time Humphrey was being nominated. This would avoid the snare of everyone being arrested in the afternoon. If they were going to make a mass arrest anyway, we could try to delay it to the time of the nomination and make them crush us visibly in front of the Hilton rather than in a remote park.

Feeling honest about the alternatives we would lay before the assembled crowd, we made our way to the bandshell about noon. Irv Bock went to a phone booth to inform his superiors of our intentions.

When we arrived, there were about 10,000 people at the bandshell, mostly an outpouring of Chicago citizens. I remember embracing Mickey Flacks, who came with her newborn baby, Mark, trusting, with so many others, that the rally would be a peaceful one. Vivian Rothstein told her she was crazy, but she wanted to be there. We began at 2:25 p.m., with people still filing into the park. Phil Ochs started singing. Dave was chairing. A few speakers from draft-resistance organizations and Vietnam Veterans Against the War were heard. I sat toward the rear with a few savvy marshals, trying to assess the large contingent of police who had arrived and stationed themselves in the corner of the bandshell area that was on the most direct route to the Hilton.

They were handing out a leaflet announcing that "in the interests of free speech and assembly, this portion of Grant Park has been set aside for a rally," then going on to warn that "any attempts to conduct or participate in a parade or march will subject each and every participant to arrest." Meanwhile, Vivian and others were distributing a leaflet appealing to the police. While I fully expected the police to continue their brutal behavior, there was nothing wrong with reaching out to their better judgment. Forty-three U.S. Army soldiers at Fort Hood had just been court-martialed for refusing "riot-control" duty in Chicago; why not some of Chicago's finest? The leaflet was poignant in its entreaty to the police:

> Our argument in Chicago is not with you.
> We have come to confront the rich men of power who led America into a war she voted against . . . the men who have brought our country to the point where the police can no longer serve and protect the people—only themselves.
> We know you're underpaid.
> We know you have to buy your own uniforms.
> You often get the blame and rarely get the credit.
> Now you're on 12-hour shifts and not being paid overtime.
> You should realize we aren't the ones who created the terrible conditions in which you work. This nightmare week was arranged by Richard Daley and Lyndon Johnson, who decided we should not have the right to express ourselves as free people.
> As we march, as we stand before the Amphitheater, we will be looking forward to the day when your job is easier, when you can perform your traditional tasks, and no one orders you to deprive your fellow Americans of their rights of free speech and assembly.

By now the convention itself was unraveling from the strain of the week's events. Many of the delegates were joining our nightly protests as they returned to the hotels. Idealistic McCarthy workers, who turned "clean for Gene" from New Hampshire to Chicago, were heartbroken, alienated, radicalized. The effort to nominate their hero was only a matter of going through the motions. On this night, Hubert Humphrey would inevitably be nominated, the wheels of the party machine relentlessly turning regardless of the political consequences. However, a spirited fight would be taking place over the Vietnam platform plank in the afternoon. The Johnson-Humphrey position would prevail numerically, but the size of the peace bloc would measure how far the antiwar movement had reached into the Democratic mainstream.

Suddenly there began a commotion by a flagpole situated between the bandshell and the police line. A shirtless teenager was climbing the pole toward the flag. Although their hearts never seemed to melt when we sang "America the Beautiful" or "This Land Is Your Land," nothing seemed to madden the police more than affronts to the American flag. On this occasion, the teenager on the flagpole intended to turn the Stars and Stripes upside down, an international distress signal, though no one knew his intention at the time. Led by Rennie, our marshals headed over to keep order. A column of police waded in with clubs to make a forcible arrest. A few people threw stones and chunks of dirt at a police car. Dave urged calm over the microphone. The vast majority remained in their seats as Carl Oglesby, the SDS president, was introduced. Carl was an extraordinary orator, and was saying that while we tried to give birth to a new world there were "undertakers in the delivery room," when thick lines of police, clubs in position, began forming in front of the flagpole, facing off against our marshals, who had largely succeeded in calming people down. Rennie later remembered taking the megaphone and telling the police it was under control, we had a permit, and they should pull back to avoid further provocation. "On that last word," Rennie said, "they charged."

The police started forward in unison, then broke ranks, running and clubbing their way through the marshals and into the shocked people sitting on their benches. Human bodies flipped over backward. Others staggered into the benches and fell. Some police stopped to beat again and again on their helpless forms, then moved forward into the screaming, fleeing, stumbling crowd. Tear gas was wafting into the air, and I saw Mickey Flacks running off with her baby's face covered. The police were the Gestapo to her. She approached several of them, screaming, "Here, do you want the baby? Take him, take my baby!" Gaining her control, she began shuttling injured demonstrators to the university hospital on the south side, with the baby asleep in a backseat carrier.

Somebody yelled to me that Rennie was hit and lay bleeding, trampled, and unconscious. Oglesby kept speaking, describing the police state unfolding even as he tried to exercise his freedom of speech and assembly. I was not disguised, so I took my shirt off to change my appearance for the moment. Then I piled up several park benches to slow the charge of the rioting police. Next I circled around the melee toward the flagpole area to check on Rennie. He was being attended to by our medics and readied for an ambulance. His head was split open and blood was flowing over his face and down his shirt. The man standing over him with a microphone and tape recorder, I later learned, was from naval intelligence. Rennie was taken to the hospital by our own medics. Within a short while, the police arrived at the hospital to arrest Rennie, who was beginning to recover from a concussion and abrasions. The hospital staff hid him under a sheet, rolled him on a gurney through the police lines, and placed him in a cab. He was driven to South Kimbark, where he watched the rest of the night's events from the Flacks's couch, his aching head heavily bandaged.

Somehow the insanity subsided after half an hour. The police pulled back to their original position, but now they were reinforced by new units and helicopters from every direction. National Guardsmen were moved into place by the band shell as well, also taking up visible positions on nearby bridges and the roof of the Chicago Art Institute. Bleeding and disoriented from the gas, we were now surrounded on all sides. A full force of 12,000 police, 6,000 army troops with bazookas and flamethrowers, and 5,000 National Guardsmen with "Daley dozers" stretched from the bandshell back to the Hilton and the Loop.

Surprisingly, the rally went on, with Allen Ginsberg, Dick Gregory, and several other speakers. But eventually it came to a final focus. Dave Dellinger announced that there were options for people: first, joining himself in a nonviolent parade attempting to go to the amphitheater; second, staying in the bandshell area; and third, moving out of the park for "actions in the streets." He then introduced someone from the Peace and Freedom Party who made the out-of-place proposal that we go picket with the striking Chicago transit workers. Next came a bizarre Jerry Rubin, with a live pig, which he wanted to enter in nomination for the presidency. A little flustered by these suggestions, Dave reiterated that his proposed nonviolent march would begin in the far corner of the park, and then he introduced me. I was reaching a climax of anger and, curiously, freedom. It didn't matter what happened now. "Rennie has been taken to the hospital, and we have to avenge him," I began, repeating it twice to get people's attention. I pointed out the police, guardsmen, and droning helicopters, and warned that we were now surrounded as twilight approached. I urged people not to get trapped in the park, to find their way out and back toward the Hilton: "This city and the military machine it aims at us won't allow us to protest in an organized fashion. So we must move out of this park in groups throughout the city and turn this overheated military machine against itself. Let us make sure that if our blood flows, it flows all over the city, and if we are gassed that they gas themselves. See you in the streets."

Seconds later, I disappeared from the park with Bob Ross, heading for my Kimbark apartment and a new disguise. A *New York Times* reporter drove with us. I heard on the car radio that the Vietnam peace plank was rejected by the convention by a 1,500–1,000 margin and that a protest rally had begun on the convention floor. In about an hour, I was back at the band shell with a fake beard and helmet to cover my face. It was late in the day, perhaps five o'clock. Dave's march of over 1,000 people was half-sitting, half-standing, blocked by a line of police who would not let them out of the park. Meanwhile, individuals and small groups of demonstrators were headed north along the lakeshore looking for a bridge to cross onto Michigan Avenue and access routes to the central downtown area. Each of the crossings was occupied by troops employing mounted machine guns and the "Daley dozers."

By some miracle, our trotting, winding crowd finally came to an open bridge at Jackson Boulevard, north of the Loop, and with a great cry of liberation ran over the short space and into Michigan Avenue, turning left to head the mile back toward the Hilton. There were over 5,000 people cheering, running, shaking fists or making V-signs, flowing like a peasants' army toward the emperor's castle. As we headed down Michigan Avenue, the mule-drawn Poor People's Caravan, which Dr. King had intended to lead before his death, materialized seemingly from nowhere, with Ralph Abernathy leading it. It was 7:30 p.m., nearly time for Humphrey's nomination. The streets were open, as the police were forced to regroup in the face of our surprising initiative. The Dellinger march disintegrated, and everyone found their way toward the Hilton.

It was nearly dark as we reached the corner of Michigan and Balboa, where all the swirling forces were destined to meet. Lines of blueshirts were in front of us, clubs at the ready. The protest column filled the street and swelled with unity as we moved straight ahead. The first lines sat down.

As if by magic, hands were aloft in the evening air, and we began chanting, "The whole world is watching! The world is watching! The whole world is watching."

We saw smoke and heard popping noises a split second before tear gas hit our front lines and began wafting upward into the Hilton and nearby hotels. We stopped, choking, trying to bite into our shirts. Then the police charged, chopping short strokes into the heads of people, trying to push us back. They knocked down and isolated several people, leaping on them for terrible revenge. One very young demonstrator was caught in the gutter, four or five police cutting his head open with clubs. A reporter took a famous picture of him, face bleeding, holding up the V-sign, before he passed out. Medics wearing Red Cross armbands, who tried to get to him and others, were clubbed, choked, and kicked down in the street. Mace was squirted in the face of any others who approached, including the photographers. The mass of people fell back, stunned but orderly, helping the injured, to regroup for another march forward.

Bob and I got through the front lines and around the police to the very wall of the Hilton, where a mixed group of fifty or so McCarthy workers, reporters, protesters, and—for all I knew—plain ordinary citizens, were standing frozen against the wall, between the hotel and the police. When the marchers fell back, the police turned on our trapped crowd, moving in with a vengeance, clubs and Mace pointed at our faces. We instinctively joined arms. They started pulling off one person at a time, spraying Mace in their eyes, striking their kidneys or ribs with clubs, and tripping them. Their eyes seemed to be bulging with hate, and they were screaming with a sound that I had never before heard from a human being. Someone started shouting that a woman was having a heart attack. We were so besieged that I couldn't turn around to see what was happening. Then, as people started staggering backward, someone kicked in the window behind us, and we fell through the shattered street-level opening to the Hilton's Haymarket Lounge (named, strangely enough, in memory of Chicago police killed by an anarchist's bomb during a violent confrontation between police and protesters in 1886). The police leaped through the windows, going right by me, turning over tables in the swank lounge, scattering the drinkers, breaking glasses and tables.

Now, the inside of the Hilton was a battleground. Trapped demonstrators were trying to sit inconspicuously—in Levi's and ripped shirts—in chairs in the lobby until it was possible to get out safely. Bloody victims were walking about dazed, looking for help, as bellboys and clerks stared in shock. Reporters were rubbing their heads and trying to take notes. The McCarthy forces started bringing the injured to a makeshift "hospital" on the fifteenth floor, where they had head-quarters. It had been a very bad night for them. The candidate's wife Abigail and children were warned by the Secret Service not to attend the convention; she assumed this was because they could not be pro-tected from the Chicago police.

Upstairs now, the staff members of the defeated presidential can-didate were ripping up bed sheets to serve as bandages. Many of the wounded were their own. Some flipped-out political aides were throw-ing hotel ashtrays at the police down in the street; others were trying to pull them away. Lights all over the McCarthy floors of the Hilton were blinking on and off in solidarity with the protesters in the streets below. Soon, the police cut the phone lines to the McCarthy suites and, in a final orgy of vengeance, stormed the fifteenth floor, dragging sleeping volunteers out of bed and beating them up as well.

At the convention, Humphrey was being nominated, but not with-out resistance. Senator Abraham Ribicoff, in nominating Senator George McGovern, stated that "with George McGovern, we wouldn't have Gestapo tactics on the streets of Chicago." Mayor Daley, in the first row, was interpreted as screaming, "Fuck you, you Jew son of a bitch, you lousy motherfucker, go home!"

After Humphrey's nomination, which took until midnight, the McCarthy contingent vowed to march back to their hotels. About 3:00 a.m., we welcomed them, a funeral column of tie-wearing delegates, each somehow holding a candle against the foul night air. Robert Kennedy had been fond of quoting a Quaker, saying in his brief pres-idential campaign, "Better to light a candle than curse the darkness." Now it had come to this: while I welcomed these candles in the park, I wanted to curse the darkness.

I had reached exhaustion; so had the protest. So too had the hopeful movement I had hoped to build only a few years before. Over the course of the next day, the defiance wound down. Halfway to the Amphitheater, a march led by Dick Gregory was stopped by more arrests, this time of many convention delegates themselves. We heard Eugene McCarthy, with gentle dignity, urge us to "work within the system" to take control of the Democratic Party by 1972. He was harangued embarrassingly by SDS leader Mike Klonsky as a "pig opportunist." Ralph Abernathy spoke from an impromptu stage, an upside-down garbage can, calling it a symbol of Martin Luther King's last cause.

I lay on the grass, pondering the alternatives. Reform seemed bankrupt, revolution far away. We had taught the pro-war Democrats the lesson that business as usual was a formula for political defeat and moral self-destruction. But was anybody listening?

I felt drawn into a tunnel of our own, with no light at its end.

The National Commission on the Causes and Prevention of Violence, appointed by President Johnson, concluded that a "police riot" was to blame for the disaster. In his introduction to the report, *Los Angeles Times* reporter Robert J. Donovan described the Chicago police behavior as nothing less than a "prescription for fascism."

Drawing on 20,000 pages of witness statements, most of them from the FBI and the U.S. Attorney's offices, and 180 hours of film, Walker's team came to conclusions at great variance from Daley's accounts. There were 668 arrests during Convention Week, most of them involving individuals under 26 years of age, the vast majority being young men from Chicago with no previous arrest records.

About 425 persons were treated at the movement's makeshift medical facilities. Another 200 were treated on the spot by movement medics, and over 400 received first aid for tear gas. A total of 101 required treatment in Chicago hospitals, forty-five of those on the climactic night of August 28.

There were twenty-four police windshields broken, and seventeen police cars dented (by whomever). In addition, 192 of 11,000 officers checked themselves into hospitals. Of this number, 80 percent were injured in the spontaneous events at Michigan and Balboa on August 28. Only ten police, according to their own affidavits, said they were kicked, six said they were struck, and four said they were assaulted by crowds.

In contrast, of 300 press people assigned to cover the street actions, sixty-three (over 20 percent) were injured or arrested. Fifty (including Dan Rather) were struck, sprayed with Mace, or arrested "apparently without reason," in the words of the Walker Report. The Daley machine had tried to sharply limit television access to the convention and streets; when that failed, allowing the whole world to watch their tactics.

When the convention was over, Richard Daley offered his personal explanation for the violence in an interview with Walter Cronkite. Rennie, Dave, and I were communists, he darkly hinted, and that somehow explained it all. The mayor's words recall the blind mendacity of those times:

DALEY: Well, there really isn't any doubt about it. You know who they are.

CRONKITE: No, I really don't actually.

DALEY: Well, you know Hayden, don't you, and what he stands for?

CRONKITE: I don't know that he's a communist.

DALEY: . . . You sure know Dellinger, who went to Hanoi. Why don't, why isn't anything said about these people? They're the people who—go over now, see if your cameras will pick them up in Grant Park. Rennie Davis. What's Rennie Davis?

CRONKITE: Well, I don't know that they're communists.

DALEY: Well, neither do I, but . . .

I suppose it was fitting that such a bad year would end with the election of Richard Nixon to the presidency. The Democrats never recovered from the convention cataclysm and, more fundamentally, from Vice President Humphrey's continued allegiance to Lyndon Johnson. In retrospect, it is almost inexplicable that Humphrey did not distance himself from the president until late in the campaign, and then ever so timidly. The president's long-standing position was that there could be no American bombing halt without a "reciprocal" North Vietnamese military response. On September 30, Humphrey proposed an unconditional halt of bombing to clear the way for diplomatic process, though he reserved the right to resume the air war. Immediately, there was a subtle shift of new support toward Humphrey. As Theodore White's history noted, there were no antiwar hecklers after that. A newspaper photo showed a student with a sign reading IF YOU MEAN IT, WE'RE WITH YOU. The McCarthy forces began supporting Humphrey actively. At the same time, support for third-party candidate George Wallace was eroding.

The Gallup poll of October 21 showed the depth of Humphrey's problem. Richard Nixon, pledging both law and order and a "secret plan for Vietnam peace," was leading by a 44–36 margin. In late October, Hanoi agreed to sit at the same table with the Saigon regime if the bombing stopped. On October 31, with the election less than a week away, Johnson played his trump card, announcing the bombing halt. On November 2, both the Gallup and Harris surveys shaved Nixon's lead to a perilous 42–40. According to White, "had peace become quite clear, in the last three days of the election of 1968, Hubert Humphrey probably would have won the election."

There has been much political conjecture that Hanoi wanted a victory at the American ballot box. Yet if any Vietnamese party meddled in American politics in 1968, it was the Saigon regime. By all accounts, they hoped for a Nixon victory to improve their bargaining position. As several histories of the 1968 election have indicated, staunch Republicans, such as Mrs. Anna Chennault, intervened to persuade General Thieu, on behalf of candidate Richard Nixon, not to join the new Paris talks. Hold out for a Nixon presidency, they implied, and a better strategic position. Thieu agreed, and Johnson's peace initiative fell through at the last minute.

Nixon's victory was by 0.7 percent: 43.4 percent to 42.7 percent.

The movement that had begun on the back roads of Mississippi saw its dreams napalmed by Vietnam; similarly, we who proposed political realignment found ourselves after 1964 and 1968 still excluded from a Democratic Party that meanwhile upheld such affronts to peace and justice as allowing segregationist Mississippi senators to remain entrenched as chairmen of the Judiciary and Armed Services committees in America's highest legislative body. Mississippi blacks had been excluded in 1964; now the entire reform wing of the party was out in the streets. Emotionally scarred by eight years of battle, politically convinced that the party was beyond reform, I found it unimaginable that in just four years there would be a triumph of reform, that George McGovern would be nominated or that Richard Daley would lose his status as a convention delegate. My belief in the system was in critical condition

Rarely, if ever, in American history has a generation begun with higher ideals and experienced greater trauma than those who lived fully the short time from 1960 to 1968. Our world was going to be transformed for the good, we let ourselves believe not once but twice, only to learn that violence can slay not only individuals, but dreams. After 1968, living on as a ruptured and dislocated generation became our fate, having lost our best possibilities at an early age, wanting to hope but fearing the pain that seemed its consequence.

As Jack Newfield wrote, after 1968, "The stone was at the bottom of the hill and we were alone."

Demonstration at the Federal Building in Chicago during the conspiracy trial.

THE TRIAL: 1969–1970

A successful prosecution of this type would be a unique achievement of the Bureau and should seriously disrupt and curtail the activities of the New Left.

—J. Edgar Hoover, October 23, 1968

CHICAGO POLICE DEPARTMENT **Intelligence Division** **March 27, 1969**

Captain Kinney (Newark police intelligence) called to relate that a meeting was held in New York City . . . by attorneys who will represent the eight demonstrators indicted by the Federal Grand Jury . . . The following information was obtained at this meeting:

1. Attorneys are taking the attitude that the demonstrators will be convicted and will work to force error on the part of the judge in order to get an appeal.

2. An attorney from New York named Weinglass will attempt to discredit the judge sometime during the trial.

3. The defendants will attempt to turn the proceeding into a circus and will wear false faces during at least one day of the trial. . .

This information was telephonically forwarded to Assistant U.S. Attorney Richard Schultz.

THE SCENE: The twenty-third floor of the Chicago Federal Building, a black steel tower shielded from natural light and air by its green-tinted windows. It is September, a brisk, gray season in Chicago that turns soon into the bitter cold winter on the windy shores of Lake Michigan.

Leaving the elevator on the twenty-third floor, one is confronted by federal marshals, about a dozen of them keeping order in the hallway. Spectators trying to get into court start to arrive at 5:00 a.m. and wait outside in the cold. Then they will have to leave their coats and belongings on the hallway floor, pass the inspection of the marshals, and hope they will be among the few who get in. Otherwise, they must begin again another day. Once successful in getting into the courtroom, if spectators had to leave for any reason, they were subject to losing their seats. Often they were forced to leave when they broke the rules by gasping or laughing. For these "crimes," many of them were beaten. The thudding of fists and the screams of pain became part of the pattern of insanity.

The courtroom is a square chamber with mahogany walls, carpeted floor and an entire ceiling of fluorescent lights. At the sides are doors leading off to the jury room, the judge's private chambers, and next to the defendants' table, a corridor of gray stone cells. In the front is the Great Seal of the United States, and just beneath it is the tiny, bespectacled, hairless head of Judge Julius J. Hoffman. The head moves in a regular bobbing motion, perhaps from a nervous tic, or perhaps because of the judge's years, then being 73. The head, which is all we could see of the judge, is elevated about ten feet above the floor. Behind it are several framed portraits of America's Founding Fathers.

Judge Hoffman is known to his friends as "strict," and to most observers as a "hanging judge." (Years after the trial, in 1976, Hoffman was rated as "unqualified" by 78 percent of the lawyers polled by the Chicago Council of Lawyers. But in 1969, his Chicago critics confided that they could never openly protest what they called his imperious behavior for fear of losing future cases before him. Protected thus from lawyers' criticism, the judge was further insulated from the ferment of the 1960s by a conservative lifestyle. A Republican, he was a resident of the exclusive Gold Coast area of Chicago overlooking Lincoln Park. Through marriage, he was the millionaire beneficiary of stock in a defense firm, the Brunswick Corporation, which had been the target of antiwar pickets in 1968.)

Below and slightly to the right of Judge Hoffman is the neat table of the prosecution. There sits the main prosecutor, U.S. Attorney Thomas Foran, whom Rennie had approached unsuccessfully in 1968, asking that Foran appeal to Mayor Daley for permits. Foran was in a unique position to know Mayor Daley, having once been his appointee at City Hall for land acquisition (known to irate community groups as the "urban removal" program). Foran is a former Golden Gloves boxing champion and a veteran who flew over one hundred bombing missions in World War II. Short and muscular, his curly hair turning gray, he has a rasping tone of voice, which develops an edge of disgust when referring to us. He expresses little emotion, though he endlessly clicks the end of his ballpoint pen. Foran's assistant district attorney, Richard Schultz, is a younger man, a year older than I am, a driven legal professional. While Foran is a man of political leanings and ambitions, Schultz is computer-like, fascinated with details, collecting and sorting alleged facts into the grand design of conspiracy. (He would study FBI transcripts of my speeches, for example, until two or three in the morning. "I would get absorbed in it because it was beautifully written and argued," he told me many years later. "Then I would snap out of it.")

Both Foran and Schultz were themselves on the streets of Chicago in 1968, in liaison roles between the federal authorities and the Chicago police. Schultz was on the very spot where demonstrators, including me, fell through the windows of the Hilton's lounge on August 28. Both were aware that Attorney General Ramsey Clark opposed convening a grand jury to seek criminal conspiracy charges. After Nixon's election, Foran and Schultz visited the new attorney general, John Mitchell, and in Foran's words, "really liked his legal mind." They gave serious thought to not indicting us, they claimed, only because of the platform we would be provided. But, in the last analysis, they pursued the indictments because otherwise it would appear that we "got away with it." In Foran's theory, keeping us "sitting on a needle" would bring the movement to an end. To this day, they deny any conspiracy of their own with the judge or FBI to control the trial to their benefit, and they remain convinced of our absolute guilt.

Perhaps with this goal of "ending the movement" in mind, they targeted as defendants eight individuals from Chicago in 1968 who represented the varieties of radical dissent: Rennie and I were the New Left, Abbie and Jerry the counterculture, Dave Dellinger the conspiratorial antiwar network and Bobby Seale the Black Panthers. John Froines and Lee Weiner, the only two of us who were not symbols of larger movements, were indicted for their alleged lawbreaking as Mobe marshals and were the only defendants completely acquitted by the jury. In addition, it appeared that women *sui generis* were not considered dangerous or subversive, since none were indicted—an omission that actually angered several women who thought they were as qualified for prosecution as any of the male defendants.

We were charged technically with a conspiracy to travel over state lines for the purpose of "fomenting a public disturbance" involving three or more people in "actual or threatened" violence. For each defendant, there was one count of conspiracy and one count of inciting violence, each carrying five-year penalties. The charge of conspiracy is well known as a prosecutor's dream because it requires no evidence of actual meetings, actual decisions, or actual implementation of a plan of violence. Thus, it didn't matter that several of us in this conspiracy had never met each other before being in Chicago, or in the case of Bobby Seale, before being indicted. All that was necessary was providing a *pattern* in our actions implying a collective "intent." The charges erased the traditional meaning and protection of the First Amendment. The well-defined freedoms of speech and assembly, as we understood them, allowed a citizen to *advocate* any doctrine, no matter how offensive or revolutionary. Such advocacy could not be considered criminal unless connected directly and tangibly with the *carrying out* of the idea in violation of personal or property rights. The classic formula of the courts was that freedom of speech ended when one cried "Fire!" in a crowded theater.

But according to the law under which we were prosecuted, a new limit on freedom of speech would be introduced. Our *prior* speech was to blame for *later* violence—even if we were not present at the violence itself, and even if it happened months later without our knowledge or will.

For instance, one item of evidence introduced against Dave Dellinger was a speech given on July 12, 1968, one month before the convention, in San Diego. Present was a paid FBI informer, Carl Gilman, who took notes on Dellinger's one-hour talk. His notes were inexplicably destroyed, but Gilman testified that Dellinger said: "Burn your draft cards. Resist the draft. Violate the laws. Go to jail. Disrupt the United States government in any way you can to stop this insane war." Assuming these were Dave's exact words, they were perfectly legal, however shrill, by usual understandings of the First Amendment. His speech was not followed by any illegal action; it was pure advocacy. The only statement about Chicago, according to the FBI agent, was a comment at the end of the speech in which Dellinger allegedly stated, "I am going to Chicago to the Democratic National Convention, where there may be problems." The speech ended with applause, then Dellinger said, "I'll see you in Chicago." The "problems" in Chicago which Dellinger referred to in his speech, the agent testified, were related to the anxieties demonstrators felt over the nature of their welcome to the city. On such a thin thread of evidence was the giant web of violent conspiracy woven.

Another example was a speech by Rennie in Cleveland on August 17, 1968. This talk, recorded by another FBI informer, made no mention of violence or disruption aimed at the convention, the government, or any other institution. In fact, Rennie was quoted as saying:

> We want to say here in Cleveland that our fight is not with the policemen, not with the National Guard troops, our fight is not with the young men who are being ordered in Fort Hood, Texas to come to the convention for the protection of that convention from its own citizens. Our fight is with the *policies* of the United States government that have created this situation . . .

Even though Rennie described in some detail the agenda and program of entirely legal activities for the week, the prosecutors singled out one phrase: "the anger and militancy will be strongly expressed to the governing party and the world."

There were three speeches on which the prosecution depended to prove my guilt. The first and second were given in New York City, in March and July respectively. At the first one, notes were kept by Louis Salzberg, a photographer of twenty years with full press credentials, who had been receiving between $7,000 and $8,000 yearly from the FBI for photographing demonstrators. Salzberg's testimony was that I had said we would "fuck up" the convention. But he confessed to have burned his own notes and claimed the words *fuck up* were not included in the typewritten version of his report to the FBI because the agency had "young girls as stenographers, and they will not print them that way." In addition, he acknowledged that I expressed hope that there would be no riots in Chicago and that a Yippie speaker accompanying me had stressed that our purpose was not to incite violence at the convention.

The second New York speech, in July, was on the subject of the Vietnam War and the Paris peace talks. Listening this time for the FBI was Frank Sweeney, a New York advertising man who had been approached to become an informer by an FBI neighbor at a Little League game. Sweeney made no notes until an hour and a half later, when he paraphrased the speech while waiting for a bus. He remembered that I had called for "shedding blood" and "breaking the rules." What I in fact had said was that we had to be "prepared for shedding *our own* blood" and that the "rules of the game" of politics were rigged and ought to be broken.

The third speech was the spontaneous one from the Grant Park stage on August 28 after Rennie had been beaten, the crowd clubbed and gassed, and the park surrounded. This speech, the prosecution claimed, led to the mass demonstrations in front of the Hilton some four hours later. In one sense, they were right. But I had hardly crossed state lines intending to give such a speech. The key question was who provoked the violence that night. On this point, the Walker Commission was clear: the police themselves had rioted.

The thought of finding the complex truth about Chicago by targeting eight individuals as scapegoats was absurd from any investigative point of view. Conspiracy theories, after all, are self-fulfilling. They ignore as irrelevant the underlying causes that lead individuals to rebel. They deny that riotous behavior can occur spontaneously. Using informers for evidence virtually guarantees that phrases or sentences will be taken out of context and blame focused on single individuals. From Mississippi to Chicago, the establishment had always externalized its own responsibility by claiming "outside agitators." Lyndon Johnson had been cited in several histories as believing that international communist conspiracies lurked behind the American antiwar movement.

"The substance of the crime," Judge Hoffman said one day, was a "state of mind." The phrase was close to that of Deputy Attorney General Richard Kleindienst, who labeled people like us as "ideological criminals" who should be placed in detention camps. Going further, Attorney General John Mitchell boasted in those years, "We are going to take this country so far to the right you won't even recognize it." Moreover, I believed, there would be expanded wiretapping and other forms of intrusion into civilian, democratic life by the FBI, CIA, and military intelligence, perhaps even preventive detention, denial of bail, and roundups, as happened to radicals in 1920 and to Japanese Americans during World War II. Certainly, I expected Nixon's appointees to the higher courts to be staunch conservatives, dimming our prospects of successfully appealing a verdict in Chicago. Leonard Weinglass told me before the trial to expect a legal railroading and a ten-year sentence. If I drew "good time" as a model prisoner, he said, I could be out in seven years. In my anxiety, I imagined prison riots behind bars, even death, as did happen later at Attica State Prison in New York.

Rennie Davis, William Kunstler, Tom Hayden and Charles Garry at defense attorneys' offices during pretrial meetings, spring 1969. NACIO JAN BROWN

Our choice for defense attorney was Charles Garry, the Panthers' general counsel. We accepted Garry primarily because he was the incarcerated Bobby Seale's personal lawyer, and also because of his general reputation for brilliance in defending unpopular clients. An Armenian by birth, Garry was a silver-haired San Franciscan who put himself through law school at night in the 1930s. He was also a wise man in the up-and-down history of the Left—perhaps too much so. When we first met with him soon after the indictments, he said he was sure one of us was an agent. I don't know if it was said simply for effect or to indicate how coldly and carefully he would handle the case if he entered. The second thing he said was that he would only enter if he could be chief counsel and make all the final decisions. He also lectured us against any outbursts or disrespectful behavior in the conduct of the trial. If there was, Garry said, we could all "go to hell." In the light of the later history, it might seem amazing, but we all agreed.

But we also wanted a hand in picking the other lawyers who would be part of the defense team. My personal choice was Leonard Weinglass; even though he'd never handled a federal case, I thought he had the sensitivity and courtroom skills to win any jury. The Yippies were worried that Len was too "straight" and inexperienced and was only a friend of mine (although they later turned to him for aid during every major crisis of the trial). They wanted, and we all gladly agreed, to have William Kunstler, a civil rights attorney who had argued many cases in the South. Then in his late forties, Kunstler was located at the Center for Constitutional Rights in New York, and he was a close associate of my Newark friend Morton Stavis. If Garry was the king of skillful cross-examination and novel defenses, Kunstler got by less on technical skills than on righteous oratory. Len was slated to be the key technician of the three, preparing witnesses, organizing the order of the defense case, researching points of law, and constructing appeals on the judge's rulings.

Then on September 9, two weeks before the trial began, there came a hearing that changed everything. Charles Garry was in a San Francisco hospital, recovering from an emergency operation on his gall bladder. He sought a six-week postponement in the trial, and submitted a doctor's affidavit indicating precisely how long recovery would take. For some reason, the judge adamantly refused, setting the stage for the crisis which was to come. "We don't characterize anybody as chief lawyer or just plain Indian lawyer," he declared, in clear violation of any defendant's right to be represented by counsel of his choice. This was particularly true in the case of Bobby Seale, facing not only Chicago charges but a Connecticut murder trial, locked in jail every night without contact with the outside world. Bobby had been driven to the trial by marshals, in chains, all the way across the country despite a court order in San Francisco against his removal. He had every reason to want Garry's guidance for his daily defense.

Bobby was fundamentally different from his image as an American Mau Mau. The real Bobby was an angry and inflammatory person, to be sure, but he also exuded a humanity, keen powers of observation, a sense of humor and a desire for simple decency behind his mask. Not all the Panthers were as responsible as Bobby. I remember one meeting at the Oakland Panther headquarters where a minor political disagreement led to a Panther security guard strangling me until Bobby stopped him. This was not a party of gentlemen. Bobby was three years older than I was, came from a rough home life, was discharged from the Air Force for a "bad attitude," attended Merritt Community College in Oakland, worked as a draftsman and mechanic, and most enjoyed being a stand-up comedian. When Malcolm X was killed in 1965, Bobby went into a rage and threw bricks at police cars; but the same Bobby worked on community relations and federal antipoverty programs in North Oakland for the next year. He became the right-hand man of Huey Newton, whom he called the "baddest nigger ever," and when Huey went to jail, Bobby was left to represent and run the whole organization himself, which by that time, was growing by leaps and bounds. One month before the Chicago trial began, while leaving an Oakland wedding, he was arrested on conspiracy charges involving the murder of a suspected black informant in New Haven, charges that were eventually dropped. Slapped in handcuffs that night in Oakland, he was driven all the way to Chicago by federal marshals to stand trial with the rest of us while the Connecticut charges were pending. He was awakened at Cook County jail each day at 5:00 a.m. and brought to the courtroom. Local Panther leader Fred Hampton, a 21-

year-old, hardworking organizer, built like a halfback and wearing a broad smile, brought messages to Bobby faithfully every morning in court and made calls on his behalf during the day. In addition, a black law student named "Mickey" Leaner kept the Panther leader supplied with legal citations regarding the constitutional rights of black Americans, which Bobby carefully wrote into his yellow pads. In refusing to grant the six-week postponement, the judge tried to claim that Bobby was amply represented by Kunstler, Weinglass, and several other attorneys who had only appeared to argue pretrial motions.

At the time, I thought, rivalries between the Garry and Kunstler camps were contributing to a failure to solve the problem. Garry didn't want Kunstler to represent Bobby or other Panthers and was insisting that Bobby go to trial without a lawyer. I could understand Bobby's need for Garry, but I feared it would make matters worse if he had no lawyer at all. The cunning Garry was hoping for a declaration of mistrial to separate Bobby from the rest of us, thinking he could vindicate Bobby more easily in a later trial without the seven of us involved. He could show that the Panther leader was in Chicago for less than one day and knew virtually none of the defendants at the time. But that, I thought, would be dividing the defendants along race lines and against ourselves. A lesser evil would have been to let Kunstler go ahead and defend Bobby with the rest of us. But there was no persuading the Garry office. They gave strict instructions for Bobby simply to stand on his right to counsel of his choice.

And so on opening day, after each of the lawyers for the prosecution had made opening statements, Bobby rose and walked to the lectern in front of the judge. Asked who his lawyer was, Bobby said, "Charles R. Garry." Foran jumped up, demanding the jury be removed from the room, which it was, and then a profound argument between Bobby Seale and Julius Hoffman began. Seale politely but firmly insisted he had constitutional rights, under the nineteenth-century Reconstruction amendments, to the legal defense of his choice. The judge pointed out that Bobby had a "very competent" attorney in Bill

Kunstler. Then Bobby drew the lines clearly: "If I am consistently denied this right of legal defense counsel of my choice by the judge of this court, then I can only see the judge as a blatant racist of the United States court."

"What's that, what's that?" the judge replied, startled. Then he launched into the first of many nostalgic remarks about past newspaper editorials praising him for his liberal decisions on desegregation in the 1950s. They were at loggerheads, Bobby having a protected right he refused to compromise, the judge inflexible about a setting a new date for starting the trial.

When the trial finally opened, Hoffman escalated his attack on the lawyers. As we began, Kunstler stated for the record once again that not all the defendants were fully represented because of Charlie Garry's absence. Prosecutor Foran claimed that not only were we represented by Kunstler and Weinglass, but that our several pretrial lawyers should be brought in. We, of course, refused, and so the judge promptly issued bench warrants for Gerald Lefcourt in New York and Michael Tigar, Michael Kennedy, and Dennis Roberts in California. They were picked up by marshals or turned themselves in, arrested for not agreeing to defend us in court. The judge again tried to bargain the defense into accepting Kunstler instead of Charles Garry, even telling Kunstler, "You can give them the key to the county jail." The threat was refused, and so the pretrial lawyers were thrown in jail and given contempt citations. According to Tigar, in whose empty room I had stayed when I hitchhiked to Berkeley in 1960, Foran said, "If you don't convince Bobby Seale to drop his right-to-counsel claim, we're gonna hold you in Cook County jail all weekend, where you can get your white asses raped." Instead, the pretrial lawyers were granted bail by a higher court, and when hundreds of lawyers poured into Chicago to protest from around the country, the four pretrial lawyers were released from the judge's order.

The jury selection process gave other ominous signs of things to come. When we first saw the roomful of hundreds of people from whom our jury of twelve "peers" would be drawn, I felt as if I were at a convention of the Silent Majority. There were virtually no young people, almost no people of color, no one not registered to vote (since the names were drawn from voter lists). Weinglass made a motion, to no avail, that a true jury of peers would have to include a broader cross section of people than these. Then we got down to the rough task of choosing the best people possible from this unrepresentative assemblage. To make matters worse, the judge would allow no questions of the prospective jurors except concerning their job and family status. We could ask nothing about whether they harbored feelings about Convention Week, the Vietnam War, blacks, long hair, or anything that would indicate an ability to be objective.

The judge began by reading the indictment to the room of jurors, relishing and emphasizing every phrase about "rioting" and "incendiary devices," until Kunstler stood and objected to his reading the charges "like Orson Welles reading the Declaration of Independence." When our turn came, we tried a different sort of appeal to the jury, having Weinglass declare that we regarded the eventual twelve people selected as the "highest authority" in the courtroom, a legal principle that is well grounded if little used. The judge, furious at the implied challenge to his own authority, stopped Len short. But we weren't indulging in a gesture; from the beginning, we knew the jury was our only hope. We scarcely entertained the possibility of an acquittal; there were too many charges and too many defendants for everyone to be found innocent. What we really feared was that the government had created the ingredients for a jury to reach a "compromise" verdict sentencing us each to jail for five years, rather than ten years. Our courtroom strategy was to achieve a "hung jury," persuade a hardcore minority to hold out for total acquittal on the permissible grounds that they had reasonable doubt about our guilt. Then, we were convinced, the government might not want to go through the negative publicity and cost of trying us a second time. The key was to select some jurors capable of maintaining their own principles to the end.

In the game of jury selection, twelve people are chosen by lottery to take their seats in the jury box. Then the prosecution and defense are allowed seventeen peremptory challenges, by which they can throw a juror out of the box without a stated reason. Next, a new juror from the large panel is chosen to fill the seat, and the guessing game goes on until one side has exhausted its peremptory challenges or both sides are happy with the twelve in the box. The government expected us to use up all of our peremptory challenges on the grounds that the whole jury panel was unacceptable to us. But we decided on a different path: to protest that the game was rigged, but then play the percentages. We would wait until a moment that Foran indicated the jurors were acceptable to him, then in a surprise move accept the same panel. We didn't need a perfect jury. We just had to be reasonably sure a handful were winnable to our point of view.

Our side was limited to staring at the faces and appearances of the prospective jurors and listening to a few of their words. We whispered, passed notes, tried to get the jurors to look at our eyes. The prosecutor removed two we thought were potentially good: a young chemist and an unemployed black electrician. But we took hope from Kristi King, a young woman with a decent face who had a sister in VISTA, the domestic Peace Corps. Then our eyes bulged at the sight of a book under the arm of the next juror: it was by James Baldwin, unusual reading material for a white Chicagoan. Mrs. Jean Fritz was a woman of about forty with a kind face. Had Foran seen that book? Was this Fritz lady trying to signal her sympathy? Or was it a trick to get the support of the defense? We asked for a break so that we could meet. It was granted, and we found ourselves arguing in a jail cell that the judge kindly made available. There were nine women and two men on the current panel, including Kristi King, Jean Fritz, and a few other possibles. But next in line was a young, sincere-looking woman named Kay Richards, whom several of us believed was on our side. If we accepted the jury as it was, we would keep King and Fritz, but Richards would only remain an alternate who would join the jury if someone got sick during the trial. If we continued the guessing game, we would get Richards into the jury box but might have Fritz or King bumped. We took a collective gamble and instructed Kunstler and Weinglass to accept the jury the way it was. When we returned to the courtroom and announced our satisfaction with the jury, Foran looked surprised and disturbed. It was a conservative, middle-American jury, but we believed we had at least two good jurors and a very good alternate in Kay Richards.

We were in for some real surprises, however.

In 1987, I talked with Jean Fritz and one of her daughters at length about her impressions of the trial. She was still living in Des Plaines, a Chicago suburb, with her husband of fifty years, Marvin, a tire-store owner. Her three girls, Nancy, Margie, and Janice, were all grown up, and she and Marv were spending their new leisure time fishing and generally enjoying life. It had taken her a long while, however, to get over the Chicago trial, and she shared with me what it was like, week to week, for a Middle American like herself.

When she took the elevated train to Chicago for jury duty that morning, she carried the Baldwin novel simply to keep her mind stimulated. She had followed the riots of 1968 through the media and felt the accused conspirators were a "bunch of jerks." Little changed her opinion as she sat for hours through the jury selection process that day and the next. She remembered getting on an elevator with Abbie Hoffman and thinking, "God, why doesn't he take a bath?" Those were the times, as she recalls, "when even soap was out." Her opinions were shared by the other jurors. "No one was sympathetic to the defendants. We were just a bunch of middle-class people who only knew what we read in the papers."

A few days later, as the trial's second week began, the judge announced that "threatening letters" had been sent to two of the jurors, including Kristi King. The letters, both written in the same hand and mailed from the same place, simply said, "You are being watched" and were signed "The Black Panthers." Bobby and the rest of us immediately suspected a right-wing plot to discredit the Panthers and knock one of our best jurors out of the box.

The incident allowed the judge to make two serious decisions. First, he sequestered the jury, putting them under permanent supervision of federal marshals for the rest of the trial at the Palmer House Hotel, instead of at home with their families, where they could feel free, read and hear the news, and, we thought, be more able to understand our case. "We couldn't even know about the moon landing!" Jean Fritz remembered. "When they walked us from the Palmer House to the Federal Building, we couldn't even look in the windows. I almost had a fight with one of the woman sergeants." At night, the jurors watched endless James Bond movies, courtesy of the marshals.

Second, the judge used the alleged Panther letters to remove Kristi King from the jury. It was totally unnecessary, because she had never seen the notes herself. They were received by her parents, who turned them over to the FBI. The judge brought her alone into the jury box and asked her to read one of them. She said she had never seen it before. Then the judge announced that it had been sent to her and demanded to know if she could still be impartial. Her face reddened, she looked in shock over at Bobby Seale, paused in confusion, and said, "No." She was immediately removed. Our intuition that she was on our side was later confirmed by Jean Fritz. The other juror who received a letter, Mrs. Ruth Peterson, said she had already read and discussed the letter with another juror (which was improper in itself) and could remain impartial. The young alternate, Kay Richards, was now added to the jury. We felt that was a plus, but we questioned the bogus letter and demanded that the court order a full investigation. The judge agreed to our request. However, I was more convinced than ever that the real conspiracy was not among the defendants but on the government's side. It was very difficult to believe they were following their duty not to communicate among themselves. I didn't know how they were conspiring, but I believed that the judge of the district,

William J. Campbell, a former law partner of Mayor Daley, was linked to Judge Hoffman and perhaps to Foran himself. Later FBI documents strongly hinted that this was so.

FBI MEMORANDUM

[Assistant U.S. Attorney] requested letter sent to Peterson family and King family be examined for latent fingerprints. He desired absolutely no other investigation or outside contacts at this time. No investigation should be undertaken without contacting him or the USA. Judge Hoffman concurs.

Kay Richards "was for Foran 100 percent from the beginning," Jean Fritz said later. "She kept questioning all the other jurors about their opinions, because she said she was writing a book. Her boyfriend was Tom Stevens, who worked somehow for Mayor Daley. She was always talking about him, and after the trial, she married the guy."

FBI MEMORANDUM   10/7/69
TO: DIRECTOR
FROM: SAC, CHICAGO

As the Bureau is aware, with appropriate Bureau authority and with security guaranteed by the SAC, SA's have monitored and, where possible, recorded speeches at public gatherings by the defendants, as well as some of their supporters.

The United States Attorney (USA) Thomas A. Foran and the presiding judge at the captioned trial, the Honorable Julius Hoffman, are concerned that the defendants will claim on appeal of any conviction in captioned case that defendants could not receive a fair trial due to the publicity surrounding the trial. Judge Hoffman and USA Foran must be in a position to prove that the publicity was caused

by the defendants, their lawyers, and their associates rather than the government. In addition, Judge Hoffman has indicated to USA Foran, and USA Foran is in full agreement, that many of the statements made by the defendants, their lawyers and possibly others such as the unindicted co-conspirators, may well be in contempt of court. *Judge Hoffman has indicated in strictest confidence that following the trial he definitely plans to reconsider various individuals for possible contempt of court* [emphasis added].

Our state of mind and behavior cannot be understood apart from the serious events that were taking place *outside* the courtroom. Nixon's pledge of a "secret plan" to end the Vietnam War looked more and more like a deceitful escalation. The president's goal was to reduce American casualties while increasing the number of Indochinese deaths, on the cynical assumption that most Americans would not care about body counts of people of color. Under the "Vietnamization" policy, about 60,000 American troops were being withdrawn by the start of the Chicago trial. American combat deaths for 1969 were down by one third, from a high of 14,592 in 1968 to an eventual 9,414 in 1969. Recorded Vietnamese deaths were ratcheting upward, not winding down; between 1969 and the end of 1973, Saigon army losses increased by 50 percent, to 250,000, and civilian casualties in the South alone by 50 percent, claiming another 1.5 million people. United States figures for enemy deaths in South Vietnam in 1969 were 157,000. Later, U.S. Senate investigations estimated that four million people in Indochina were turned into refugees between 1969 and the summer of 1971. The masterpiece of Nixon's doctrine was the secret B-52 bombing of Cambodia, begun in March 1969. It was called Operation Menu, since the United States bombed a specific area designated as "Breakfast," then waited for a North Vietnamese response before proceeding with raids identified as "Lunch," "Dinner," "Dessert," and "Snack." In those raids alone, 3,650 B-52 sorties dropped four times the tonnage of bombs dropped on Japan in all of World War II.

Nixon, it is now known, was also planning a more severe escalation of the war if Hanoi did not enter productive negotiations by late 1969. Labeled "Operation Duck Hook," the proposed options included destruction of Hanoi and Haiphong, the mining of North Vietnam's rivers and harbors, attacks on the dike system to provoke massive flooding, and—if necessary—use of nuclear devices on the Ho Chi Minh Trail.

During the trial, we read the first published reports of the 1968 My Lai massacre after the Pentagon had suppressed the evidence for a year. The slaughter of hundreds of unarmed Vietnamese villagers injected yet a new sense of horror for many who thought themselves numbed to the war. The scene of women, children, and babies mutilated and dumped in a long ditch would become the *Guernica* for my generation. "I sent them a good boy, and they made him a murderer," cried the mother of one of the soldiers at My Lai. Apart from this single hideous incident, there was a systematic repression campaign, labeled "Operation Phoenix" and supported by U.S. advisers, computers and funding, which targeted the "Vietcong infrastructure" in South Vietnam—an estimated 2 percent of the population, or well over 350,000 organizers, farmers, teachers, unionists, students and women, suspected of being "national security threats." Massive arrests, interrogations, torture and outright killing took place through the Phoenix program.

Starting in 1969, the desertion and AWOL rates increased fourfold over the 1965–68 figures. In the same year, fragging (grenade assaults) against officers began, averaging 240 incidents per year, 11 percent of them fatal. Between 1969 and 1972, there were 86 officers killed and 700 injured. The U.S. Navy conducted 488 investigations of sabotage in its own ranks in a single year. Marijuana use doubled from 30 to 60 percent of all GI's in the Nixon phase of the war; more gravely, heroin addiction jumped from 2 to 22 percent. By 1971, while

5,000 American GI's would need hospitalization for combat wounds, over four times as many—20,000—were treated in military hospitals for drug abuse. In the end, 500,000 Vietnam-era veterans would receive "less than honorable" discharge papers.

The Vietnam War, in short, was destroying the American idealism of an entire generation, whether in Chicago or Saigon.

In the meantime, the protest movement at home was exploding dramatically. Suddenly, it was no longer deviant but legitimate—patriotic even—to express an alternative opinion. Just before the Chicago trial began, Abbie and Jerry attended the vast gathering of Woodstock in upstate New York, the coming of age of the youth culture. Then in mid-October, the Vietnam Moratorium—organized primarily by former McCarthy workers Sam Brown and David Mixner—became perhaps the largest public protest in American history. Precisely because it lacked militancy and a clear set of demands—"give peace a chance"—the Moratorium provided a safe channel in turbulent times for Middle Americans to step forward into the ranks of dissent. As many as ten million Americans gathered in town squares and college campuses to speak out against the war. For our part, on October 15, Dave tried reading the names of American and Vietnamese war dead and we placed American and Vietcong flags on our defense table before Judge Hoffman's proceedings commenced. But the judge and the prosecution flew into a rage, ordered us silenced and had the flags removed. Outside, during the lunch break, several of us spoke to one of the largest crowds I have ever seen at a Chicago rally. The two events together—Woodstock and the Moratorium—reflected exactly the spirit of a generation we had dreamed of expressing in the original planning for Chicago 1968. Now, one year later, the time had come.

Meanwhile, back in the dreary oppressiveness of the courtroom, the government was busy grinding out its case against the conspiracy defendants.

Juror Jean Fritz's initial dislike of the conspirators was deepened by the Yippies' defense of drugs. A friend of hers had "lost her mind" because of drugs, and she worried about her daughters. But as the weeks passed, she began having doubts about the government's case. It was not the details of testimony that affected her; it was Judge Hoffman's eccentric and arbitrary behavior. "The judge changed me a lot in the beginning," she said.

One night that winter, Rennie spoke at Northern Illinois University, just outside the city. His statements sparked a lively debate among the student audience, prompting Margie Fritz, Jean's daughter, to stand up suddenly. Her words were critical of the prosecution. When she announced that her mother was a member of the jury, the FBI agents surveilling Rennie turned their tape recorders and notebooks toward her. The following morning, Jean Fritz was called before Judge Hoffman in his chambers. She was asked if she had communicated with her daughter. An affirmative answer would have resulted in her removal from the jury. Telling the truth, she said, "No." In the prosecutors' imagination, the daughter was having an affair with Rennie. "Margie used to come to the trial when she could, and we would look at each other across the room," Jean said. "One day a marshal came up and told her that I could go to jail for six months because of what she said at the college. She became a total wreck and quit school for six months." Jean Fritz was allowed to remain on the jury.

The prosecutors brought to the witness stand a cross section of the very city bureaucrats who had denied us permits in 1968, as well as various undercover agents who swore to tell the truth. One official testified that he took seriously an offer of Abbie's to leave town in exchange for $100,000. Foran and Schultz fought to have us referred to by our last names: "Objection, Your Honor, to the familiar child terms for mentally grown men." A police agent testified that the chief act of violence he saw Jerry Rubin commit was throwing a sweater at an officer during the gassing of Lincoln Park. Another described how he joined a motorcycle gang headed by two men named "Banana" and

"Gorilla" in order to penetrate the Yippies. This police agent, who became Jerry Rubin's "bodyguard," said he witnessed Rubin throwing paint at a police car. While that was the only act of violence he recalled Rubin committing, the agent testified that he himself had taunted police as "pigs," thrown objects at them, helped rock a surrounded police car, taken drugs, picked up a gang girlfriend, and sold his memoirs to *Official Detective* magazine for one hundred dollars.

As this shady testimony droned on, we became restless and more worried. The judge was ruling in behalf of the prosecution on virtually every motion and objection. He allowed Foran to make unusually disparaging remarks about our lawyers. Foran told Kunstler, "Instead of watching yourself on TV tonight, you can study evidence." But the real edge of ugly conflict continued to be the treatment of Bobby Seale.

By October 20, three weeks into the trial, Bobby was actually permitted to argue a motion that he be allowed to defend himself. Using the research supplied him, Bobby argued not only on the grounds that citizens may represent themselves in court, but also on the specific grounds that arose after the Civil War in response to false representation of southern blacks by white lawyers, guaranteeing black people the right of legal self-defense. It was clear and well argued, but summarily denounced by Schultz as a "ploy." The government claim was that Bobby would make so many mistakes that he could appeal for a new trial. The judge even declared that the "complexity of the case" was too much for Bobby to follow, which enraged Bobby into responding: "You denied me my right to defend myself. You think black people don't have a mind. Well, we got big minds, good minds, and we know how to come forth with constitutional rights."

Being acted out was a symbolic conflict of particular importance to the Panthers, which Eldridge Cleaver had described as that in which the Supermasculine Menial is feared by the Omnipotent Administrator for attempting to assert his own equal intelligence in exposing discrimination as irrational. "The more the Menial asserts his own ideas," Eldridge wrote, "the more emphatically will they be rejected and scorned by society, and treated as upstart invasions of the realm of the Omnipotent Administrator . . . the struggle of the Menial's life is the emancipation of his mind, to achieve recognition for the products of his mind, and official recognition that he has a mind."

Bobby now embodied this struggle in the courtroom. He confined his statements to those moments when evidence specifically against him was introduced by prosecutors or witnesses. He would then object that he was without counsel and denied the right of defending himself by cross-examination of witnesses. The conflict became tense on October 28, when a police agent named William Frappolly mentioned Bobby in his testimony. Bobby strode to the lectern, stating: "I object to this testimony because my lawyer is not here. I have been denied my right to defend myself in this courtroom." The judge cut him off, suggesting that Bobby was in contempt of court for making his remarks. Bobby bitterly replied that it was the judge who was "in contempt of the constitutional rights of the mass of people of the United States. . . . I am not in contempt of nothing. The people of America need to admonish you and the whole Nixon administration." At the end of that afternoon, the judge had a chilling surprise. Obviously well prepared, he flatly informed Bobby that "under the law you may be gagged and chained in your chair."

Chains? On a black person one hundred years after slavery? Gagging? For a person who could so easily be granted the right to represent himself? We were outraged. We checked the law; such stern measures were warranted in the few exceptional cases in which a defendant had thrown chairs at the judge or witnesses, but never when one simply spoke out in court. What were we going to do? Sit there? Pretend we were going through a normal trial, making motions, examining witnesses, chatting with the press, going home after the day was done—ignoring a black defendant, bound and gagged, sitting in our midst as in a living nightmare out of the American past?

When we arrived the next morning, October 29, there were at least twenty-five armed marshals lining the walls. A few anxious Panthers and young whites sat on the edge of their seats waiting for what was to come. When Bobby was led into court, carrying his familiar yellow notepad, he smiled and returned a clenched-fist salute from his supporters. Still standing at the defense table, he made an unmistakably clear appeal for his supporters to keep order. "Brothers and sisters," he said very personally to them, "we have the right of self-defense if pigs attack us, but today let's be cool, let's be cool, whatever happens. I'm going to defend my constitutional rights and, whatever happens, be cool, and if the marshals ask us to leave, just leave." The small group replied, "Right on, Bobby," and sat down.

Minutes later, the judge entered from his chambers and before he could begin speaking, Schultz was on his feet at the lectern, almost whining. "Your Honor, Your Honor," he said, "minutes before this court was in session, the defendant Seale was addressing his followers back there about an attack by them on this court."

Bobby jumped up, yelling that Schultz was a liar, that he had urged people to "be cool," that Schultz was a "racist and a fascist" for his remarks. The judge started pounding his gavel as defendants, spectators, and even reporters shook their heads and complained about Schultz's twisting of Bobby's remarks. Meanwhile, Bobby was still demanding that Schultz apologize. Bobby then pointed to the portraits of the Founding Fathers behind the judge and asked, "What can happen to me more than what happened to the slaves under George Washington and Benjamin Franklin?" The judge reddened and told the marshals, "Take that defendant into the room in there and deal with him as he should be dealt with in this circumstance." Five or ten of them did, gouging and dragging Bobby into his chair. All of us jumped up. Dave Dellinger tried to put himself between the marshals and Bobby, getting knocked aside. Jerry Rubin got punched in the face as he yelled, "They're kicking him in the balls." I tried to get the judge's attention: "Your Honor, all he wants is to be legally represented, not be a slave here." As each of us would speak or move, the prosecutors would excitedly declare, "Let the record show," and then describe our behavior for future contempt citations. They finally got the struggling Bobby down. We continued storming around, cursing, asking each other what was going to come next.

It was a repeat in the courtroom of what had occurred in the streets of Chicago the year before. We had been accused by the prosecutor of provoking violence, triggering a cycle of outraged resistance that gave the pretext for an act of repression. The chains and gags were probably waiting in the next room for just this occasion. Now we were threatened with revocation of bail: "Since all the defendants support this man in what he is doing," the judge intoned, "I, over the noon hour, will reflect on whether they are good risks for bail, and I shall give serious consideration to the termination of their bail." We froze, refusing to rise again.

We weren't going to stand in respect for a judge who was about to crush the rights of Bobby Seale. We didn't know what to expect when we returned to court, but we instructed Bill Kunstler to give the following reply to the judge:

> MR. KUNSTLER: The defendants want me to say that under no circumstances will they let their liberty stand in the way of the assertion of the constitutional rights of Bobby Seale to defend himself, and if the price of those rights is that they must remain in jail, then that will have to be the price that is paid. Many have paid much greater prices in the past for the defense and assertion of constitutional rights.

No one in court that day will ever forget the loathsome sight of Bobby Seale being carried back into the room. Surrounded by marshals, he was sitting in a high chair with his wrists and ankles strapped under clanking chains. Wrapped around his mouth and back of his head was a thick white cloth. His eyes and the veins in his neck and temples were bulging with the strain of maintaining his breath.

As shocking as the chains and gag were, even more unbelievable was the attempt to return the courtroom to normalcy. The judge ordered the cross-examination of the witness on the stand to resume. The jury returned from lunch and sat down; one member, Jean Fritz, was visibly quaking. The press reopened their notebooks. And the judge and prosecutor became suddenly solicitous and polite to Bobby. Foran proposed that if Bobby expressed a willingness to be quiet, the court would consider un-gagging and unchaining him. The judge leaned over Bobby and lamented that he had "tried, with all my heart, to get him to sit in this court and be tried fairly and impartially." He told Bobby to indicate "by raising your head up and down or shaking your head, meaning no, whether or not I have your assurance that you will not do anything that will disrupt this trial. . . ."

To everyone's surprise, Bobby's voice pierced through the gag, forcefully though if somewhat muffled: "I can't speak. I have a right to speak. I have a right to speak and be heard for myself and my constitutional rights." The judge leaned farther over, shaking his head politely as if he were at a loud cocktail party. "I can't understand you, sir." I started to laugh in relief and admiration; they can't gag Bobby, no way. Bobby even criticized Kunstler through the gag. Bill had tried to describe the metal chair, handcuffs, and gag for the court record, and Bobby muttered through the gag, "You don't represent me. Sit down, Kunstler."

Now there was real trouble for the government. Their "quick fix" to this human problem had broken down. Embarrassed but stubborn, the judge blamed the problem on the marshals: "I don't think you have accomplished your purpose by that kind of contrivance. We will have to take another recess." They carried Bobby into the side room and this time pushed a plug-like device into his mouth before tying the cloth gag around his face. When Bobby returned, the judge again tried to resume the normalcy of the trial. We interrupted with motions for a mistrial, which were denied, and Foran went back to taking routine testimony from the witness.

By now this process had proved deeply unsettling to four of the jurors; besides Jean Fritz, they were Shirley Seaholm, Frieda Robbins, and a black woman, Mary Butler, who Jean thought was very compassionate. Mary was ill at the time and died a few years later. Each of the four women had teenage children. They became a subgroup, taking many of their meals together. "What set us off was when they did all that to Bobby Seale," Jean said later. "I'd never seen anything like that in my life, and never will again. The marshals came in the back room where we were waiting to go out, and all they told us was, something was going to be different when we went back out in the courtroom. I was shocked when I saw him."

That night, after seeing Bobby's chains and gag on national television, Bernardine Dohrn and Terry Robbins wanted to see me. I met them in a Hyde Park restaurant, and after dinner we took a long walk. They were angry that the other defendants didn't react to Bobby's chaining by trashing the courtroom and joining him in jail. By what right, she asked, were we continuing the trial with a black defendant chained and gagged? Weren't we displaying the very skin privilege that meant the black community couldn't count on white radicals?"

The questioning of my guts, as usual, was effective. I felt a certain guilt over my restraint in the courtroom. But I also knew, through a third party, that Charles Garry wanted Bobby to take his stand and punishment alone. Anything shifting the spotlight would be confusing, Garry thought, and could weaken Bobby's case ultimately.

"Look," I finally said, "I'm committed to a trial, not a riot in the courtroom. I think they have to take the gag off Bobby. They want us to tear the room up and go to jail. I think we should put on a defense, speak on campuses, get our message out, and win with the public."

Bernardine shifted her tack, replying slowly and carefully. "Don't you listen to Nixon and Agnew? Don't you understand what this judge is doing? You are going to jail at the end of this trial. What I really think is that you should split before it's over. Fascism is what's happening. I think you should go underground before they take you out."

The next morning, Len was directed to go ahead with cross-examination. But there was a scraping and clanking sound from Bobby's chair. Len stated to the Court: "The buckle on the leather strap holding Mr. Seale's hand is digging into his hand, and he appears to be trying to free his hand from that pressure. Could he be helped?" The jury was excused, and barely out of the room, when a group of marshals got into a pushing conflict with Bobby and knocked his chair over.

At once, everyone was up, and marshals were slugging and elbowing the other defendants, spectators, and even members of the press. The emotion simply exploded without any focus. Bobby was yelling through the gag that his blood circulation was being stopped. Jerry Rubin protested, "This guy is putting his elbow in Bobby's mouth," and got kneed and knocked over himself. Kunstler took the lectern tightly between his hands, and asked, "Your Honor, are we going to stop this medieval torture chamber that is going on in this courtroom?"

Everything became surreal. Now I knew how wars started.

MR. KUNSTLER: Your Honor, this is an unholy disgrace to the law that is going on in this courtroom and as an American lawyer I feel it is a disgrace.

MR. FORAN: A disgrace created by Mr. Kunstler.

MR. KUNSTLER: Created by nothing other than what you have done to this man.

MR. ABBIE HOFFMAN: You come down here and watch it, judge.

MR. SEALE: You fascist dogs, you rotten low-life son of a bitch. I am glad I said it about Washington used to have slaves . . .

MR. DELLINGER: Somebody go to protect him.

MR. FORAN: Your Honor, may the record show that it is Mr.

Dellinger saying "somebody go to protect him"—and the other comments were by Mr. Rubin.

THE COURT: Everything you say will be taken down.

MR. KUNSTLER: Your Honor, we would like the names of the marshals. We are going to ask for a judicial investigation of the entire condition and the entire treatment of Bobby Seale.

THE COURT: Don't point at me in that manner.

MR. KUNSTLER: I just feel so utterly ashamed to be an American lawyer at this time.

THE COURT: You should be ashamed of your conduct in this court, sit.

MR. KUNSTLER: What conduct, when a client is treated in this manner?

THE COURT: We will take a brief recess.

MR. KUNSTLER: Can we have somebody with Mr. Seale? We don't trust . . .

THE COURT: He is not your client, you said.

MR. KUNSTLER: We were speaking for the other several defendants.

THE COURT: The marshals will take care of him.

MR. RUBIN: Take care of him?

THE COURT: Take that remark down. The Court will be in recess.

When court resumed, the judge instructed Len to continue a cross-examination, but he couldn't. The crisis was now unbearable. Len moved that the jury be asked if it could continue to deliberate fairly while one defendant was chained and gagged. That began another eruption of objections from Foran, and at once nearly everyone was rising and arguing. Several of the defendants decided that we would tell the puzzled jury what was happening as soon as they reappeared. When they came back in the room, Rennie stood and gazed at the jury and declared, "Ladies and gentlemen of the jury, he was being tortured while you were out of this room by these marshals. It is terrible what is happening. It is terrible what is happening." The judge ordered the jury out again, and some almost ran while others moved slowly, trying to listen over their shoulders. Bobby tried to appeal to them, through his gag, and was knocked down by the marshals. I shouted, "Now they're going to beat him." Abbie snarled, "You may as well kill him if you are going to gag him. It seems that way, doesn't it?" To which the judge replied, "You are not permitted to address the court, Mr. Hoffman, you have a lawyer." "This, man, isn't a court," Abbie declared, "*this is a neon oven*. This disruption started when these guys got into overkill. It is the same thing as last year in Chicago, the same exact thing."

Somehow, order was restored again, and the judge commanded another witness to the stand. But the testimony was meaningless since all the attention was on the strapped and seething figure of Bobby. Finally, on the third day of the ordeal, Len, Jerry Rubin and I asked permission to fly out to meet Charles Garry over the weekend. We badly needed a break for a strategic discussion. Surprisingly, the judge granted the request as long as we promised not to "vilify" him on television. I said that was not the purpose of the trip, but that I would not be gagged by such an order. On Friday night we found ourselves flying to San Francisco.

As soon as we landed, rented a car, and started for Garry's house, state police pulled us over. They wanted to know if any of us intended to make statements for television or public appearances during the weekend. Slightly startled by the long arm of the Chicago law, we indicated there were no such plans and continued on. Garry and his legal team were waiting for us at his comfortable hillside house in Daly City, just south of the San Francisco city line. After we described for them what they had been reading and watching in the media, it was apparent that there wasn't anything Garry himself could do at this point. He drafted a strong statement condemning the denial of Bobby's right to self-defense, called for a dismissal of the case as "irretrievably prejudiced" against all the defendants, and concluded that "even if I were physically and medically able to take part in a major trial, which I am not according to my physicians, my participation could in no way cure the fundamental constitutional infirmity with which it is already plagued."

On Monday morning, yet another surprise awaited: there sat Bobby Seale in his chair, without chains or gag, his yellow notepad in front of him. Over the weekend, someone decided that the nationally televised spectacle of the brutalized black American had to end. But it made no sense simply to take off the shackles without resolving the central issue of his representation. Before the jury came in, the judge and Schultz once again tried to get Bobby to waive his legal claims. After Bobby emotionally objected to his cruel and unusual punishment and reasserted his determination to defend himself, Len leaned over and whispered to me, "They've decided to get rid of him. It'll be a mistrial."

He was right, but the ripe moment for the government did not come for two days. On November 4, the prosecution chose to call to the stand one Bill H. Ray, a deputy sheriff from California who had observed Bobby boarding a plan for the Chicago demonstrations in 1968. He was the only witness the government called to prove the "interstate travel" part of the indictment against any of the eight defendants. If there had been an informant at the airport, I realized, they must have been planning to indict Bobby even before he flew to Chicago to speak. As soon as the witness identified him, Bobby tried to assert his right of cross-examination. By now I felt I was watching a play with predictable characters; the only question was who had written the script and what the last act was. When the judge dismissed the jury, I sensed the climax would come right after the lunch break. Sure

enough, about 2:30 p.m. the judge entered the courtroom holding up
a thick sheaf of papers, which he began to read aloud:

> As we all know, the defendant Bobby G. Seale has been guilty
> of a conduct in the presence of the court during this trial
> which is not only contumacious in character but of so grave
> a character as to continually disrupt the orderly administra-
> tion of justice. . . . Accordingly, I adjudge the defendant
> Bobby G. Seale guilty of sixteen criminal contempts . . . There
> will be an order declaring a mistrial as to the defendant
> Bobby G. Seale and not as to any other defendants.

He looked up over his spectacles with finality. The marshals were
taking up positions all around the room, several of them removing
their badges, waiting for us to explode. The full weight of the judge's
act took a minute to absorb. All our legal research indicated that a judge
could never sentence someone to more than six months for contempt
of court without a jury trial on each count. What Judge Hoffman had
done to avoid the embarrassing possibility of sixteen separate new tri-
als for Bobby was to sentence him to three months in prison for each
contempt "to run consecutively." That would avoid the jury-trial
requirement and result in a total sentence of more than four years.

Then came a most surreal moment. After ten weeks of silencing
Bobby's attempts to defend himself, the judge leaned down to the sentenced Panther and said in a kindly and paternal voice, "You may
speak now, sir."

Bobby, startled, responded, "I can speak now, but I can't speak to
defend myself?" As the judge's mistrial order was read, Bobby looked
around and asked, "Wait a minute, I got a right—what's the cat trying
to pull now? I can't stay?" As the marshals moved toward Bobby, the
judge ordered everyone to rise and recess for the day. To scattered calls
of "Free Bobby," the marshals took him by the arms as he spoke his
last words: "I have a right to go through this trial. I'm put in jail for

four years for nothing? . . . Hey, I want my coat." Then they marched him rapidly through the side door to prison.

The trial within a trial, that of Bobby Seale versus American justice, was over. For hours, for days, we felt hollowness, as if the life of the trial had ended with the punishment and severance of Bobby. But the government went on, relentlessly introducing its witnesses, targeting the seven of us as its next victims. We realized we had a job to do, speaking to and educating a confused country about what happened to Bobby.

And somehow, we had to prepare a defense of our own to take to the jury.

Chicago Eight defendants (Bobby Seale not present) with attorneys Kunstler, Kennedy, Weinglass, and others at a pretrial meeting, spring 1969.
NACIO JAN BROWN

THE VERDICT

We became known as "The Conspiracy." The seven remaining defendants camped in apartments in the Hyde Park area near the university, about forty-five minutes from the Federal Building. Leonard Weinglass and I rented a railroad apartment; besides ourselves, a few staff members moved in during the trial. The place was barren. At night it became the central headquarters of the legal defense team. It quickly became known that Kunstler was better at giving seat-of-the-pants speeches and partying at night than at the drudgery of preparing the legal defense. Therefore, after court each day, we would spill into a local bar, drink and eat, then return to our apartment to prepare for the next day. We would often be preparing witnesses, writing memos, and arguing the case until well after midnight. We lived on junk food, coffee, wine, and bourbon. The Yippies stayed mostly to themselves in an apartment nearby, preferring marijuana and plotting their adventures late into the night as well. At our apartment, a kind of camaraderie-of-the-damned continued until we dropped in exhaustion, people often crashing on the floor in sleeping bags. Sometimes we were joined by sympathetic celebrities like Dustin Hoffman, my hero from *The Graduate*, who was interested in learning to mimic both his namesakes, Julius and Abbie. Very few friendships could blossom in these stark conditions, and many were strained and abandoned. Women in our ranks—whether they were lovers and/or "Conspiracy" staff—were especially frustrated, since all of them were forced into the classic secondary, supportive roles that their liberated feminist consciousness rejected.

Abbie, Jerry, and to a lesser extent, Rennie, were aroused by their roles as defendants, and actually dreamed of forming a permanent national organization if we survived the trial, which was developing a national television audience several times a week. I thought it was a crazy idea for several reasons: We were not likely to be vindicated; we couldn't agree among ourselves politically; our egos were blindly competitive; we were all men; and none of us had real constituencies to be accountable to. I felt that organizations like the Mobe and the Yippies were beginning to outlive any useful purposes, and we would be perpetuating little more than our own image and notoriety.

What I really wanted was a home. Almost every Friday afternoon, I caught a 5:00 p.m. plane to Berkeley, adding to my distance from the other defendants. Bur coming from the harsh, and usually freezing, reality of Chicago made forty-eight hours in Berkeley seem even more unreal. I could see Anne and a few friends, but before I could feel relaxed and close to anyone, it was time to catch the Sunday-night red-eye back to O'Hare Field. I would take a cab to the apartment, shut my eyes for an hour, shower, and leave for the courtroom again.

One weekend was a particular nightmare. The Rolling Stones were performing at nearby Altamont. I stayed home, but most of our friends went. They were full of anticipation that this would be another Woodstock, a time of good vibes and the music of revolution, but they returned a day later, shaken. Bad drugs, probably cut with speed, were being passed out free, causing people to flip out and get sick. Mick Jagger's lyrics, oozing with violence toward women ("Under My Thumb"), made one of my friends flash for twelve hours on being raped; around her, women *were* being raped. And around the prancing Jagger were hulking Hell's Angels, one of them wearing a wolf's head, serving as bodyguards. At the climax of the concert they beat up a black man and stabbed him to death. My scared friends were throwing up and taking Thorazine.

Fred Hampton, Tom Hayden and Rennie Davis in defense attorneys' offices during pretrial meetings, spring 1969. NACIO JAN BROWN

During the same few days, the Charles Manson "family" was indicted for the sadistic murders of actress Sharon Tate and others in Los Angeles. Anne and I were nauseated by the report of Tate's stomach cut open with a fork; Tate was pregnant at the time. It was the ultimate act of barbarism. But many people, including some at several underground papers, fell into the illusion that Manson was a persecuted and misunderstood hippie. Jerry Rubin was one. He and Phil Ochs went to see Manson in prison. Manson told them that he wanted to conduct himself defiantly like the Chicago Seven in his upcoming trial. Jerry was fascinated. Looking back twenty years later, Jerry told me, "In my frame of mind I wanted to believe that the charges against Manson were an FBI frame-up. I was so into romanticizing outlaw behavior that I looked for any possible explanation to find something good in the outlaw. If society had made Manson mad, then I thought that society was to blame for Manson's crimes, not Manson. And that attitude was part of the madness of the times."

That same week was the worst of the trial. On the evening of December 4, as Leonard Weinglass recalls it, the two of us were visited by Fred Hampton at our apartment. The Panther leader was jokingly known in the community as the "ice cream bandit," because of a conviction and sentencing to a two- to five-year term for helping black children steal seventy-one dollars worth of ice cream from a vendor during the hot summer of 1968. For this, the Chicago police and media described him as a "known felon." There was an aura about Fred, who had been a youth leader with the National Association for the Advancement of Colored People, and a top student and athlete at a suburban high school who made everyone smile, and he was especially supportive to Bobby in the courtroom.

Fred's ice-cream conviction had been upheld by an appeals court, which is what brought him to our door for advice. Accompanied by a Panther security guard we didn't recognize, Fred wanted to know how much time the appeal would take. He was clearly calculating whether to jump bail and go underground. If imprisoned, he expected to be killed. We held a short, whispered meeting in the hallway outside our apartment, after which Fred and his guard departed. My impression was that he was leaning toward vanishing. Though their security operation seemed fragile, a number of Panthers had already managed to go underground successfully.

Following the meeting, I rushed off to join the other defendants for a prescheduled filming of an absurdist version of the trial by Nicholas Ray, the director of *Rebel Without a Cause*. I played the role of Judge Hoffman, sitting on a platform elevated twenty-five feet in the air. Afterward, we stayed out drinking and clowning around. I ended the lost night sitting in a bathtub with a woman from the production company and did not go to sleep until after 3:00 a.m.

At 5:00 a.m. the phone rang in our apartment. I was completely dazed when I heard a staccato of startled voices: Fred Hampton and another Chicago Panther, Mark Clark, had been killed by the Chicago police. I rolled onto the floor, head in my hands. Some of the staff members living in the apartment were already weeping. I showered and came to a stony acceptance, an unemotional sense that this was reality. Driving to court, there was no feeling left in me at all.

The details of the deaths were still coming over the radio as we arrived in court. Chicago police fired eighty rounds of ammunition into the Panther apartment, killing two and wounding four. Fred was shot four times, twice in the head, and was found lying unclothed in his bed. The morning paper carried a picture of several police officers, strangely grinning, as they carried Fred's covered body out of the apartment. The official who planned the raid, Cook County State's Attorney Edward Hanrahan, announced that the police had shown "good judgment, considerable restraint, [and] professional discipline."

Over 5,000 people attended the services. It was later revealed that William O'Neal, the Chicago Panthers security chief, stationed inside Fred's apartment that night, was a longtime FBI informant. He later admitted that the assorted guns inside the Panthers' apartment, which he controlled, were "just gathering dust."

With the weight of the Panther killings around us, we had to begin mounting our legal defense against these same Chicago police. The prosecution had finished its case, calling fifty-four witnesses, all but one of them from law enforcement.

By this time, our four sympathizers on the jury were beginning to feel isolated in their sequestered world. "The rest of them hated the four of us," Jean Fritz recalled. Kay Richards continued her proselytizing against us. Jean Fritz started developing phlebitis in one leg and needed the marshals to provide her a prop on which to rest that leg in the jury box. She began going to bed early every night, sometimes without dinner.

The defense was our chance to tell the jurors and, through the media, the public our version of what happened in Chicago and why. In addition, a protracted defense would make it possible to do more speaking on campuses around the country. The genuine jury of our peers was out there, we felt, and if they found us not guilty when the judge threw us in jail, we hoped it would set off massive demonstrations to free us around the country. The court of public opinion was our only hope.

We were not interested simply in denying that Jerry Rubin threw paint, that Dave Dellinger meant something else in a speech, that undercover agents were distorting and lying; we wanted to go beyond the narrow terms of the prosecution to the larger picture of what was going on in America that motivated us to take a stand in Chicago and, in turn, what was behind the government's indictment of us. We wanted to argue that our intentions were protected by the First Amendment, that Washington and Chicago authorities conspired to deny our rights in order to prevent embarrassment during their plan for a ritualistic endorsement of Johnson's policies through Humphrey's nomination, that we were made into symbolic scapegoats to draw attention away from the real violence of Vietnam abroad and repression at home, and that we had a certain right of resistance to the precise extent that our constitutional rights were denied.

Within this consensus, there were sharp differences. I was the most cautious of the defendants, wanting to reach the jury by pursuing a thorough, rational defense, combined with a public-education campaign, stressing that a prolongation of "Nixon's war" would inevitably lead to widening political repression. John Froines seemed to take a similar view. The Yippies were advocates of disruptive courtroom theater, including deliberate contempt of court (as the judge defined it), because they felt the media image would both desanctify the judicial system and win more identification with our cause. Dave Dellinger was more inclined to courtroom defiance as well, stemming from his background of nonviolent civil disobedience and "moral witness." Rennie, in his usual role, was mediating and trying to hold all the currents together. I think Lee believed everyone was right; he kept reading the *I Ching*.

We allowed a good deal of latitude for each defendant to maintain his own style inside and outside the courtroom. We also decided that the defense would stress the antiwar and the youth-culture emphasis of our politics equally, calling both Mobilization and Yippie witnesses. I virtually became a third lawyer, working with Ann Froines. With help from others, she would labor on the phones by day and, with me, by night, identifying and flying in a parade of witnesses and preparing them to testify. It was exhausting, but it was the only way I could hold on to my rationality.

Among the 104 witnesses we called, Staughton Lynd, as a historian, explained most articulately the basis of our actions in Chicago. We identified Staughton as an expert witness on the American Revolution to draw historic parallels with the 1968 demonstrations. The judge refused to let the jury hear Staughton on the grounds of "irrelevance," and so he could only summarize for the record what he would have told the jury. Staughton said that the First Amendment "right of petition" was based on the revolutionary Declaration of Independence and therefore protected far more militant forms of expression than usually realized.

Staughton compared our actions in Chicago with the "kind of intermediate resistance which the makers of the American Revolution carried out from 1765 to 1775," such as the boycotts of imported English goods. There was a "peculiar resemblance," he noted, between Chicago 1968 and aspects of the Boston Massacre of March 1770. In 1767, in an "unheard-of event," four regiments of British troops were landed in Boston to maintain "order." The soldiers angered the townspeople and the dock workers as a potential "threat to democracy" and provoked a series of "minor scuffles and incidents." One night three years later, a group of townspeople surrounded a particular British sentry; according to Staughton, "They called him 'lobsterback,' because of his red coat, a kind of eighteenth-century equivalent of 'pig.' They threw oyster shells and hunks of ice at him, and at a certain point, he called out the Guard." The Guard indeed came out, the people kept up the name-calling, and finally an order to shoot was given, and five colonists were killed. Staughton continued:

> The British said that the soldiers had been provoked because oyster shells and lumps of ice were thrown at them. But the colonists, Sam Adams and Paul Revere, took the position that the provocation consisted in the presence of the British soldiers having turned the city of Boston into an armed camp. That's why acts of resistance, even though certainly far more than the customary speech and assembly, seemed appropriate to people like Sam Adams and Thomas Jefferson because they were responses to an oppressive situation which had gone far beyond those normal circumstances in which speech, assembly, free press and petition were adequate responses.

> It seems to me that the jury might wish to consider the entire process of the [1968] demonstration as a kind of petitioning process in which people who felt that their elected government was no longer responsible to them, who felt

themselves to be in the same position as the colonists before the American Revolution, came to Chicago to make one last direct appeal to the men of power who were assembled in the Democratic convention.

By introducing over one hundred witnesses from all backgrounds, we tried to show that the events in Chicago were not a conspiracy of a few, but a shocking encounter for many people with a police state. For testimony about permit negotiations, we had Chicago lawyers, McCarthy campaign representatives, and even U.S. Justice Department officials on the stand. On the subject of the "police riot," we had a British member of Parliament who had been sprayed with Mace, several ministers who had been called "fucking fakes" by the police, a black police officer who had heard his own colleagues chanting "Kill! Kill! Kill!" in prevention drills, and a woman medical volunteer who had heard the same chant from police at the Conrad Hilton Hotel on the bloody night of August 28. We even found the young man who had pulled down the flag on the afternoon of August 28, giving the police their pretext for charging the crowd. Angus Mackenzie testified that he had pulled the flag to half-mast because "they killed democracy." In addition to all these unknown eyewitnesses, we called authors and artists like Norman Mailer, Allen Ginsberg, Judy Collins, Country Joe MacDonald, Phil Ochs, and Arlo Guthrie; and political representatives like Richard Goodwin from the Kennedy campaign, Sam Brown from the McCarthy coalition, Congressman John Conyers, and Georgia Representative Julian Bond. The trial defense became a reenactment of the history of the 1960s.

We chose to put only Rennie and Abbie on the stand as representatives for all of us. The beginnings and conclusions of their testimonies lasted a week in each case.

We were prevented from testifying about the central question of the trial, that of "intent." For instance, Rennie and I had written a twenty-one-page strategy paper on the proposed Chicago demonstrations for a movement conference in February 1968. This paper sketched out the alternative scenarios for Chicago and bluntly ruled out the use of violence. If the paper had advocated violence, of course, it would have been the prosecution's centerpiece. But because it advocated nonviolence, the judge ruled it "self-serving" and refused to let the jury examine or even hear about it.

The judge and prosecutor eliminated key documents or testimony again and again. None of our expert witnesses—on American history, on the youth culture, on racism in the Democratic Party, or on war crimes in Vietnam—were allowed. Abbie's two books, *Revolution for the Hell of It* and *Woodstock Nation*, were blocked from the jury. A policeman who knew of the Chicago preparations for repression was excused as a witness without telling his story, as was a National Guardsman who knew of similar plans and of live ammunition being used. The Roosevelt University president who chaired the official commission on the April 1968 police suppression of a peaceful march—widely thought to be a tactical rehearsal for the August convention—was kept silent about what he knew. So was the archivist who kept all the interview data that went into the official Walker Commission report, *Rights in Conflict*, including the interviews with Foran and Schultz.

Mayor Daley made his entrance into the courtroom, complete with his own bodyguards, on January 6. It was Jean Fritz's "biggest kick." In the back hallways where the jurors waited, she recalled, "there were guys everywhere with guns." The court itself was ringed with additional marshals as if to emphasize that the mayor's attitudes toward security had not changed since 1968. None of us had ever seen him before that moment. A legendary figure, this round, red-faced, 60-year-old "Irish Buddha" was not without a certain charm. We respected his unpolished platitudes, his protection of working-class people, and his awareness of being one-of-a-kind, a museum piece. While the mayor sat in the witness stand waiting to begin, Abbie rose with a big grin and challenged him to fight it out with fists; everyone in the room, including the marshals and the mayor, burst into laughter. We called Mayor Daley as a witness, and we sought a technical ruling by the judge that Mayor Daley be considered a "hostile witness," a step which would have allowed us to do the same sort of probing cross-examination we would to a prosecution witness. No one could have been considered more hostile than the mayor, yet virtually all of Kunstler's questions were ruled out of order and the motion to have the mayor declared a hostile witness was denied, according to the judge, because the mayor's "manner had been that of a gentleman."

If that were not absurd enough, a melee broke out when someone in the spectators' section smirked at the mayor's statement that Foran was "one of the greatest attorneys in this country and the finest man I have met in public and private life." It was Frank Joyce, a defense staff member who had gone to high school with me. One of Mayor Daley's personal bodyguards literally jumped into the spectator's section. As a result, two of our trial staff people were arrested for "assaulting marshals," charges which were later dropped. The mayor's attitude and entourage had provoked another replica of the cycle of events that began in 1968. Still, we could ask him no questions.

Not long after, on January 28, former attorney general Ramsey Clark was called to the stand. He was, in some ways, our key witness, since his testimony could go to the heart of the 1968 permit negotiations and subsequent handling of the demonstrations. We had tried and failed, earlier in January, to get testimony before the jury from two of his assistants, Roger Wilkins, who met with Rennie in 1968, and Wesley Pomeroy, who was Clark's special liaison to the convention. Both would have testified that they found Rennie a flexible negotiator and the city administration, including its ally, Tom Foran, rigid and unyielding by comparison. They had written reports conveying this message to their chief, the attorney general. Pomeroy was particularly important because he had supervised security at events as diverse as the 1964 Republican convention and the 1969 Woodstock festival. He was prepared to testify that the entire convention disaster could have been prevented by different police conduct and that he had called the attorney general on the night of August 28, 1968, to say he was "ashamed to be a law enforcement officer" after seeing the police brutality in the streets. All this potential testimony was stricken by Judge Hoffman, on grounds that it was "hearsay." We argued that the government could bring in the mayor or the relevant Justice Department officials to verify or refute Pomeroy's testimony. But our arguments were pointless.

So we embarked on the delicate mission of getting Ramsey Clark to the witness stand. Leonard Weinglass, John Froines, and I flew to the suburban Virginia home of Clark and his wife, Georgia, one weekend to ask if he would testify. The former attorney general received us very cordially and warmly. Dressed in casual clothes, he offered us a snack and apologized that he had to leave shortly to visit a sick child. We sat down to interview him immediately. What surprised me was the presence of two note-taking officials from Nixon's Justice Department. Clark, as a courtesy, had notified the department that we were coming and invited them to observe. We knew the two officials would report immediately to Foran and Schultz on whatever transpired; we were happy, however, that Clark was willing to testify without "favoring any party but the truth," about his conversations with Mayor Daley, Tom Foran, President Johnson, and other cabinet officials, and with his own representatives, Wilkins and Pomeroy. It was dynamite: the former head of the Justice Department, who had declined to seek indictments against us, explaining why he disagreed with the approach of the new department in Washington.

After this efficient and useful discussion, we left the room briefly to wash up and confer on whether anything remained to be asked. When I returned to Clark's study, the two Justice Department officials were intently talking to him by the fireplace, urging him not to be a witness for the defense. I was shocked, but I stepped back to let the encounter unfold. Clark held his ground, saying he didn't know if his testimony would be accepted, or whether it would help the prosecution or defense, but he intended to go ahead in the interests of the whole truth being available. I sensed an unbreakable commitment under his seemingly neutral and cautious phrasing.

When Ramsey Clark arrived in Chicago to testify, he was kept entirely out of the jury's sight while Schultz got up to argue that he should not even be sworn in. We again had underestimated the extreme lengths to which the prosecution would go in order to protect its case. Never to my knowledge in the history of American jurisprudence had defendants been denied the right of bringing a witness to the stand— not to mention a witness who was a former attorney general. Schultz nearly leaped to the podium, his hands full of notes made by the Justice Department officials at Clark's home. "Nothing he could say would possibly be admissible," Schultz declared with a rising tension in his voice. "According to the Code of Federal Regulations," Schultz said, "disclosure of Justice Department material was prohibited without prior approval of the attorney general—John Mitchell." The rule referred to the control of certain kinds of documents, not to the muzzling of former attorney generals. As Kunstler pointed out to Judge Hoffman, "If the regulation were interpreted as Mr. Schultz obviously would like it interpreted, this would mean that nobody in the federal government could ever testify after having left the federal government."

The judge faced this dilemma: how could the accused in a trial be prevented from calling whomever they wanted to the witness stand? He claimed discretion on the grounds that we had previously attempted to "inject irrelevant and extraneous evidence," citing the example of Mayor Daley, who "was called with much fanfare but was able to give virtually no evidence that was material to this case." Of course, the judge could protect Mayor Daley from questions, but it would be bad form indeed to "protect" Ramsey Clark from our questioning. Finally, the judge agreed to have Ramsey Clark take the stand, outside the jury's presence, to determine what Clark would say—an unprecedented "screening" of a witness's testimony.

Clark entered the courtroom, more than puzzled about what was occurring, and took the stand. Although his subsequent testimony was all but completely objected to by the prosecution, he still penetrated the screen with some small bits of information. On the assessment by Roger Wilkins of the prospects for negotiations, Clark testified that Wilkins "didn't feel that we were likely to get the cooperation that we hoped for and that the attitude from the mayor's office didn't seem conciliatory." By contrast, Clark said, Wilkins had been "favorably impressed" with Rennie Davis "as being a sincere young person." He related that a meeting was held shortly before the convention in the Oval Office of the White House to discuss the pre-positioning of troops, but the prosecution successfully objected to Clark's sharing what he advised the president. Finally, Clark was able to testify that on August 30, 1968, two days after the convention, he spoke by phone with Foran and instructed him that only a factual investigation would be made of the convention events, rather than a grand jury investigation—implying that he had no intention of prosecuting.

It wasn't even close to all Clark could say, but it was significant. Yet upon hearing the proposed testimony, the judge flatly ruled out bringing Clark before the jury. It would be a "needless delay of this trial," the judge announced. The former attorney general, dismissed from the court, melted tight-lipped through the reporters and puzzled spectators. We were instructed not to mention anything about the incident in front of the jury. It was as if the highest law-enforcement official of the previous administration was not only a nonwitness but a nonperson. The *New York Times* editorialized that this was "the ultimate outrage in a trial which has become the shame of American justice."

We definitely weren't going to accept this suppression quietly, no matter what the judge had instructed. The only question was which defendant was going to take the contempt to let the jury know. For a change, I was more than glad to do it. I sat quietly, secretly enjoying the search for the proper moment. A few days later, Foran made one of his many remarks about the irrelevance of the defense testimony, and I blurted out as the jury was leaving the room, "*You* should talk. You wouldn't even let Ramsey Clark testify for us." For that the judge sentenced me to six months, the maximum for a single count of contempt. We also attempted to subpoena one of the most shadowy figures in the Chicago case, FBI Director J. Edgar Hoover, who, we were convinced, was actively and illegally involved in harassing protestors throughout the 1960s and during the Chicago events of 1968. We wanted to compel by subpoena any information about illegal surveillance, informers, provocateurs, or wiretaps used during Convention Week. We also wanted to reveal, however difficult it was, that Hoover's agency was behind a widespread pattern of political repression against all sorts of citizen groups in America. Not surprisingly, Judge Hoffman ordered our subpoena quashed. What we didn't know was how closely the court and the FBI were collaborating.

FBI MEMORANDUM   **12/7/68**

TO: MR. DE LOACH
FROM: A. ROSEN

As a result of our discussions with the Department [of Justice], the Department has instructed the US Attorney in Chicago to immediately file a motion to quash the subpoena that has been served for the Director in this matter and William Campbell, Chief US District Judge in Chicago, has advised the Special Agent in Charge (SAC) that he will insure that the subpoena is quashed.

A copy of the subpoena was immediately brought to the attention of the Director . . . "The Director's statement 9/18/69 before the National Commission on the Causes and Prevention of Violence has been reviewed . . . No reference is made to any of the defendants or co-conspirators of the Chicago trial or to any type of electronic or physical surveillance. SDS is described as being composed of radi-

cals, anarchists, communists and malcontents with an almost passionate desire to destroy the traditional values of our democratic society and the existing social order . . . the protest activity of the New Left and SDS, under the guise of legitimate expression of dissent, was described as creating an insurrecting climate which has conditioned a number of young Americans to resort to civil disobedience and violence. The above comments in no way relate to the subpoena."

Page 27, last paragraph of the statement expressed agreement . . . that the media will highlight "police brutality" and ignore or minimize premeditated and provocative acts of demonstrators. Paragraph two, Page 2, states: "it is a tribute to the authorities that the Convention was not disrupted, the city was not paralyzed, not one shot was fired by police at demonstrators and not one life was lost. It is conceivable that the defense might attempt to utilize these statements during direct examination . . . and to provide a basis for probing the sources of information disseminated by the Bureau to local authorities."

With regard to the request in the subpoena for data relating to surveillances . . . it would be physically impossible . . . To comply would require the most extensive file search throughout the field . . . Since the Chief US District Judge in Chicago has given his assurance the subpoena will be quashed, it does not appear to be justified to instigate such a gigantic project at this time.

The winter days blurred into each other; the judge ordered us to continue the case on Saturdays, and our frustration grew as February and the end of the trial approached. There was one more vindictive insult to withstand before the final day: the revocation of Dave Dellinger's bail. As the trial unfolded, Dave had gradually lost his patience. Either from despair or a Quaker sense of direct action, he began reacting vocally, often eloquently, at outrages in the courtroom. Sometimes the situation was absurd, as when the judge ordered us to go to the bathroom in an adjoining cell instead of the public facility in the hall. Jerry Rubin and Schultz got into a heated argument with each other, and the marshals moved in. Dave said, "Don't touch him," and was ordered by the marshals to "shut up." Dave replied, hurt, "You don't have to say 'shut up.'" At other times it grew out of frustration. On January 14, for example, the judge erroneously accused Dave of saying something, to which Dave replied, "That's a lie." The judge, aroused, declared that he had "never sat in fifty years through a trial where a party to a lawsuit called a judge a liar." That stirred Dave's deepest philosophical convictions, and he rose up: "Maybe they were afraid to go to jail rather than tell the truth, but I would rather go to jail for however long you send me than to let you get away with that kind of thing." (Neither judge nor prosecutor knew the intensity of Dave's feelings. A lifelong pacifist, he went to jail for his beliefs in World War II; when released, he was asked to sign a new document making him eligible for the draft again. He refused, turned around, and served another year until the war was finally over.)

Close to the end of our defense, on January 30, the judge stopped the proceedings to announce that "one of the defendants" had given a speech in Milwaukee criticizing the judge's handling of the trial. It was Dave. The judge warned that another such speech would result in termination of bail.

A week later, on February 4, Dave lost his composure entirely. Chicago's deputy police chief, James Riordan, was testifying about Dave's role on August 28, the day that Dave stood at the front of the blocked, nonviolent march near the band shell. Riordan claimed an "unidentified speaker" told the marchers to break into small groups and disrupt the Loop and that Dave went off with a group carrying Vietcong flags, falsely suggesting that Dave had engaged in the later violence.

"Oh, bullshit," Dave blurted out from the defense table. Was that

Dave? I asked myself. Now he was angrily appealing to the witness, "Let's argue about what you stand for and what I stand for, but let's not make up things like that." It was the pretext the judge needed. He excused the jury and terminated Dave's bail without hearing arguments from our attorneys. Dave walked out the door, the oldest of us, suffering from all sorts of stomach ailments, to live out the rest of the trial in Cook County jail, waking up at 5:00 a.m. each morning to arrive in court on time.

We figured he was only about a week ahead of the rest of us.

That night the remaining defendants had the bitterest argument of the trial. Abbie and Jerry wanted to force the judge into revoking all our bail the following morning. Solidarity with Dave would be the declared reason, but they also wanted to end the trial with us already in jail. They were not just arguing, they were ranting and raving around the table at the Chicago office of the American Civil Liberties Union where we had many of our meetings. We were fast unraveling as a group. I felt that deliberately acting to have ourselves thrown in jail would only persuade people that we were intentionally trying to stop the trial through disruption and would shift a crucial degree of support back to the judge. I wanted the trial to climax around the final summations to the jury and a nationwide series of rallies or militant actions organized from our Chicago office while the jury was out deliberating its verdict. We were unable to resolve the issue, finally breaking up and going off in the grimy, cold Chicago night to decide individually how to act the following day.

The next morning, Abbie and Jerry appeared in court wearing black judge's robes covering blue Chicago Police Department shirts. Even I had to applaud their sense of theater. They were definitely intent on going to jail, but by one of the paradoxes of the trial, the judge proved unwilling to exploit their loud, defiant tactics. Abbie even started needling the judge in Yiddish: "You *schtunk. Schande vor de goyim*, huh? (Fronting for the gentiles, huh?)" He told Hoffman, "Stick it up your bowling ball," and asked, "How is your war stock doing, Julie?"

Jerry Rubin screamed at him, "You are the laughingstock of the world, Julius Hoffman, the laughingstock of the world. Every kid in the world hates you, knows what you represent." The judge acted as if they were not there and instructed the lawyers to finish their case.

His ultimate vengeance was coming.

On February 10, the summations began. All the testimony was over, all our words were spoken, all our energy was now concentrated on the appeals to the jury. Our lawyers would try to frame the case in historical perspective.

It was a duel for the souls of the presumed minority of jurors favoring our case. The prosecutors would be happy with convictions of most, if not all, of us. The indictment was structured to promote just such an outcome, with two charges against each of seven defendants. The government needed to persuade our potentially sympathetic jurors that a compromise verdict was the best they could hope for. That would still mean five-year (instead of ten-year) sentences for most of us.

It was now exactly a decade since four black students began the sit-in movement in Greensboro, North Carolina, trying to awaken and challenge their own parents' generation and the conscience of America. My decade of struggle had had the same purpose: to end the apathy of the 1950s, to make the Constitution and the Bill of Rights mean something, to put ideals into practice, to reach my parents. As I looked into the unexpressive faces across the courtroom, I realized that the jury was a microcosm of the same America that taught me to think and speak out and then broke my heart. If only a minority of the jury, even one of them, believed in our innocence and would take an absolute stand on that belief, the government would be thwarted. A hung jury would free us, and the government would be faced with the decision of trying a very unpopular case all over again. Not only would we prevail, but the government might be deterred from bringing future conspiracy cases against other dissenters.

The approach of Foran and Schultz was to combine themes that would solidify their hardcore stand on the jury while wooing our sympathizers as well. Schultz's job was to weave together the fragments of evidence into the cloth of conspiracy. He tried at length to restore the credibility of the government's main witnesses, all undercover agents, while reciting the charges against us in one compressed outpouring. With all these accusations, he was implying that we must have done something. It was Foran's task to focus on the greater themes of the case. Opening on a note of populism, he called us "intellectuals" and "sophisticated men" and "well-educated." And "you know," he flattered the jurors, "many men will be highly intellectual and yet they will have absolutely terrible judgment." Then he tried to seal us off from legitimate protesters and from leaders like Martin Luther King or Robert Kennedy. We were "liars" and "obscene haters" and, above all, "as evil as they can be." We were trying to prey on lofty causes and the innocence of young people to legitimize violence and destroy America. "There are millions of kids," he continued,

> who, naturally, resent authority, are impatient for change . . .
> They feel that John Kennedy went, Bobby Kennedy went, Martin Luther King went—they were all killed—and the kids do feel that the lights have gone out in Camelot, the banners are furled, and the parade is over. . . .
> And there is another thing about a kid, if we all remember, that you have an attraction to evil. Evil is exciting and evil is interesting, and plenty of kids have a fascination for it. It is knowledge of kids that these sophisticated, educated psychology majors know about. These guys take advantage of them. They take advantage of it personally, intentionally, evilly, and to corrupt those kids, and they use them . . .
> The lights in that Camelot kids believe in needn't go out. The banners can snap in the spring breeze. The parade will never be over if people will remember, and I go back to this

quote, what Thomas Jefferson said, "Obedience to the law is the major part of the patriotism. . . . Do your duty."

"Foran was speaking to *me*, looking at *me*," Jean Fritz said. "I was scared of them. Of what they were going to do to me. To Margie." Leonard Weinglass began our summation by trying to puncture the factual case presented by Schultz, by quoting an old legal maxim: "You can create in a courtroom anything that you have witnesses for." He then tried to reinforce the jury's likely suspicion of police agents and government informers:

> Doesn't the Government have the obligation to present before you the whole truth? Why only city officials? Why only policemen, undercover agents, youth officers and paid informers? In all of this time, couldn't they find in this entire series of events that span more than a week one good, human, decent person to come in here to support the theory Mr. Schultz has given you?

By contrast, he reminded the jurors, we brought in a variety of citizens, McCarthy people, pacifists and revolutionaries, authors, performers, religious people, medical workers. He asked the jurors if those people "could all be fooled, could all be tricked, could all be duped as the government is suggesting they were." He then pointed out that, though we had been tracked and trailed for a week, nothing more violent than throwing a sweater had been reported against any of us by the government's witnesses.

Having tried to persuade the jurors that their own government might lie, Len then confronted the social prejudice that lay at the heart of the indictment. He blamed the government's behavior on an overall failure to understand the new generation's sensitivities. For an example, Len pointed to the government's cross-examination of Allen Ginsberg, when Foran only asked if Ginsberg wrote poems about homosexuality, as if that were enough to discredit his whole testimony.

> These men are attempting to first get us to confront the real-
> ity of what life is about, and then attempt to get us to do
> something about it. It is not something that is scribbled on
> the walls of a bathroom like the way Mr. Foran reads it. To
> take it out of context and to make it sound dirty and bad is
> just reaching too far to gain a conviction.

My throat was dry as Len spoke; his argument was very personal and very challenging to the jurors' attitudes about themselves and the younger generation. By now my own former ignorance had given way to an awareness of the gay issue, but I sensed that Foran had been effective. Outside the courtroom, Foran had told his audiences that they were losing their children to the "freaking fag revolution."

Then Len shifted to a no less emotional ground, trying to reverse the conservative interpretation of patriotism. "The government's case," he said, tried to picture us as "men who bear hatred for their country, who are clearly unpatriotic, men not worthy of your consideration." He reminded the jury that Abraham Lincoln of Illinois once did "what no other congressman has done since or before: he introduced a resolution condemning the Mexican War as immoral and illegal." For that action, Lincoln met such public scorn that he was defeated in his bid for reelection. "It seems to me that if the lesson of the country teaches anything, it is that the true patriots are the people who take a position on principle and hold to it." The basic issue of the case, Weinglass concluded, was

> whether or not those who stand up to dare can do so without
> grave personal risk, and I think it will be judged in that light
> and, while you deliberate this case, history will hold its breath
> until you determine whether or not this wrong that we have

been living with will be righted by a verdict of acquittal for the several men on trial here.

Bill Kunstler asserted that because we were right, we were being martyred. "But," he asked, "could the jurors connect all the martyrs of the past, once scorned but now respectable, with the disheveled, disrespectful, angry group sitting across from them today? Or would the jump involve too much reexamination of American history, too much reexamination of their own daily assumptions about the rightness of 'law and order?'" Kunstler quoted the Chicago attorney Clarence Darrow, defending radical dissenters fifty years before:

When a new truth comes upon the earth, or a great idea necessary for mankind is born, where does it come from? Not from the police force, or the prosecuting attorneys, or the judges, or the lawyers. Not here. It comes from the despised and the outcast, and it comes perhaps from jails and prisons. It comes from men who have dared to be rebels and think their thoughts. And what do you suppose would have happened to working men except for these rebels all the way down through history?

In conclusion, he laid the responsibilities of history before this jury of twelve people, who, as far as we knew, were never before faced with decisions affecting history and politics. I watched their impassive faces as he made the final appeal, overstating our historic importance in his usual way:

You can crucify a Jesus, you can poison a Socrates, you can hang a John Brown or a Nathan Hale, you can kill a Che Guevara, you can jail a Eugene Debs or a Bobby Seale. You can assassinate a John Kennedy or a Martin Luther King. But the problems remain. . . . The hangman's rope never solved a single problem . . . . And perhaps if you do what is right, perhaps Allen Ginsberg will never have to write again as he did in the poem "Howl," "I saw the best minds of my generation destroyed by madness," and perhaps Judy Collins will never have to stand in any courtroom again and say as she did here, "When will they ever learn? When will they ever learn?"

And so it ended. "We're gonna win every day until the last," Abbie had joked with reporters. Now with the jury gone to deliberate, the juggernaut of punishment went into gear. To the surprise of many, the judge announced that he would immediately begin sentencing the defendants for their contempts of court. We were going to jail even before the verdict was in! There was little time to prepare, but an electric excitement went through everyone in the courtroom as the judge proceeded to read from an enormous memo already outlined for him. He started with Dave Dellinger, finding him in contempt thirty-two times, a sentence of two years, five months, and sixteen days. "Mr. Dellinger, do you care to say anything? I will hear you only in respect to punishment."

Dave rose slowly, already tired from two weeks in the county jail. He tried to reply to the specific findings of the judge, but was stopped once more by the command to speak only "to mitigate his punishment." Dave reacted sharply, suddenly gaining the eloquence he desired for a final statement:

> You want us to be like good Germans supporting the evils of our decade and then when we refused to be good Germans and came to Chicago, now you want us to be like good Jews, going quietly and politely to the concentration camps while you and this court suppress freedom and the truth. And the fact is that I am not prepared to do that . . .

The marshals started moving in on Dave, at the judge's instructions.

You want us to stay in our place like black people were supposed to stay in their place, like poor people were supposed to stay in their place, like women are supposed to stay in their place, like people without formal education are supposed to stay in their place, and children are supposed to stay in their place and lawyers are supposed to stay in their place . . .

The marshals came closer, grabbing Dave's arms.

People will no longer be quiet. People are going to speak up. I am an old man and I am speaking feebly and not too well, but I reflect the spirit that will echo throughout the world . . .

"Take him out," the judge commanded. There was an uproar in the spectators' section, and I saw Dave's 15-year-old daughter Michelle, red-faced, screaming, a crying tiger being held around the throat by a marshal. Her father tried to move toward her. Both were held from each other by a dozen marshals. Everybody in the courtroom was standing. Reporters were crying. Bill Kunstler collapsed over the lectern, weeping and asking to be punished next:

My life has come to nothing, I am not anything anymore. You destroyed me and everybody else. Put me in jail now, for God's sake, and get me out of this place. Come to mine [my sentencing] now, Judge, please. I beg you, come to mine. Do me, too. I don't want to be left out.

The judge indicated Kunstler would have to wait; when the jail door closed on Dave, it was Rennie's turn. Twenty-three contempts, for a sentence of two years, one month, nineteen days. Rennie too tried to speak in defense of his actions. "You may not believe this, but we came here to have a trial with a law that we regarded as unconstitutional and unfair, and a jury that was inadequately selected. We came here, nevertheless, to represent our full case to this jury . . . ."

The judge silenced him also for not speaking to the subject of his punishment. Rennie tried to explain the circumstances that led to those acts which were being judged as "contempt." The judge would not let him talk about the chaining and gagging of Bobby Seale. Rennie finally blurted out all his anger: "Judge, you represent all that is old, ugly, bigoted, and repressive in this country, and the spirit at this defense table will devour you and your sickness in the next generation." Then he too was gone, behind the door.

Strangely, we then recessed for lunch. Those of us not already sentenced were free to do as we liked. Then we would return, of our own free will, to be placed in jail. Safe citizens at lunch, convicted criminals by the afternoon. As I walked out of the Federal Building for possibly the last time, I had no sense of gravity. I hugged the supporters outside and looked for my girlfriend. She had traveled from Berkeley for the ending. We walked off to an obscure, basement-level delicatessen and bar frequented by poor people and skid-row denizens, where we avoided the press and other spectators.

When court resumed, I was next to be sentenced. The judge delivered my sentence: eleven counts, it would be one year, two months, thirteen days. Did I have anything to say with respect to this punishment? I did, and I stood up at the defense table.

> The problem for those who want to punish us is that the punishment does not seem to have effect. Even as Dave Dellinger was taken away for two years this morning, a younger Dellinger fights back. Your threat of punishment has not silenced our protest, and will not stop people from demonstrating or speaking their minds. It only fuels the protest. So, Your Honor, you have been seeing before your eyes the most vital ingredient of your system—punishment—collapsing. The system does not hold together.

Offered this intellectual challenge, the judge could not resist interrupting: "Oh, don't be so pessimistic. Our system isn't collapsing. Fellows as smart as you could do awfully well under this system. I am not trying to convert you, mind you." He was playing with me even as he prepared to send me to jail.

"The point I was trying to make, Your Honor, is that I was thinking about what I regretted about being punished. The only thing that affected my feelings," I stumbled, "that affected my own feelings, was that someday I would like to have a child." I bit my lip.

The judge leaned forward, smiling cruelly. "Well, there is where the federal prison system can do you no good."

"But the federal prison system will do you no good in trying to prevent the birth of a new world, Judge." I picked up my notebooks full of defense testimony, patted my fellow defendants, felt my eyes welling up, and marched unescorted through the door to jail.

While I sat in a holding cell, Jerry Rubin was sentenced to two years, twenty-three days; John Froines to six months, fifteen days; Lee Weiner to two months, eighteen days; and Abbie Hoffman, for reasons no one could explain, to only eight months. Our lawyers were judged severely, although they were allowed to remain out of jail to continue their work on the case. Kunstler received twenty-four citations and a sentence of four years, thirteen days; and Weinglass, whose manner was continually polite and correct, was nonetheless cited fourteen times for a sentence of one year, eight months.

As soon as we arrived at the Cook County jail, the officials cut off our hair, particularly relishing Abbie's long locks. It was a "scalping of hippies." The hair was triumphantly displayed at a press conference by Sheriff Joseph Woods—the brother of President Nixon's personal secretary, Rosemary, later to become famous for eighteen minutes of missing presidential tapes during the Watergate hearings.

The jury was still deliberating, totally unaware that we already were in jail. According to Jean Fritz, our sympathetic jurors would never have found any of us guilty if they knew the judge had already put us in jail.

While we waited for the verdict, we were paired up and placed in small six-by-twelve-foot cells among the other prisoners. We were the only whites in the jail, as far as I could see. We were minor celebrities among the prisoners, but there was a moderating recognition that we were special, privileged, that with all the publicity we would surely get out of jail. Most of these men were in jail simply because they could not afford pretrial bail; many would serve as much time in jail before trial as they would serve if found guilty and sentenced. One night, as I was lying on the floor to keep cool, a prisoner's voice from the next cell started asking me questions about our case. "Are you those white boys who burned their draft cards?" the voice asked. I said, no, not exactly, but that we knew and supported some young men who did that. "Man, I'd like to burn my birth certificate," my neighbor responded.

The jury deliberations dragged on. There were a couple of false alarms when the jury returned to court to ask further questions about the indictment. "We asked for more information," Jean Fritz said. "Two or three times, we told them we could not agree on a verdict. But the marshal kept coming back in, saying, 'You have to keep deliberating.'"

We spent hours arguing what the delays meant, hoping for a hung jury. Then suddenly we were assembled for the drive back to the courtroom early on the morning of the fifth day of jury deliberations.

Almost as soon as we sat down, the judge and marshal announced that a verdict was ready. Schultz moved that all wives and family be removed from the court before the verdict was read, and the judge concurred. The marshals swept the court, and for a final time, we sat in our chairs while our friends and family were banged, shoved, and pulled off their benches and through the doors. Schultz smugly pointed out "for the record" that "we have in the hallway now the same kind of screaming we had in the courtroom." Then the jury entered.

From the moment we saw their faces, we knew the verdict would not be good. Jean Fritz was ashen, her face lined. The jury foreman, Edward Kratske, a streetcar conductor who looked something like

Mayor Daley, handed the verdicts to the marshal, who in turn passed them to the clerk for reading. Dave, Rennie, Jerry, Abbie, and myself were found not guilty of conspiracy, but guilty of incitement. John Froines and Lee Weiner were acquitted on all counts. They were free, but they cried at the separation.

We were hustled back to jail to await sentencing. That day's press carried stories that alternately cheered and depressed us in our cells. It seemed as if demonstrations and riots were breaking out all over the country in protest against the verdict. The first interviews of the jurors showed that four members felt we were totally innocent. Why, we wondered, had they voted for the compromise verdict instead of sticking with their consciences? Foran said the verdict proved that "the system works." Vice President Spiro Agnew called it "an American verdict."

The foreman of the jury, Kratske, was welcomed home by his wife and poodle, presented with a new color television and a bowl of oxtail soup. He declared, "I've seen guys, real bums with no soul, just a body—but when they went in front of a judge, they had their hats off. These defendants wouldn't even stand up when the judge walked in. When there's no more respect, we might as well give up on the United States." What had that to do with whether we were guilty of crossing state lines to incite a riot in 1968? Nothing, I realized, and everything.

On two occasions the jury sent a message to Judge Hoffman that they were hopelessly deadlocked. "But," according to Jean Fritz, "the marshal came back in, saying, 'You have to keep deliberating.'" Jean thought the judge would keep them locked in the jury room indefinitely. The judge never answered the jury's notes. This improper pressure from a marshal apparently had its effect, and the jurors went back convinced that they had to arrive at a verdict.

By the third and fourth day of jury deliberations, Jean Fritz and the other three jurors favoring acquittal could not sleep. They felt a severe, hostile pressure to concur in a guilty finding. Fritz said later that had she understood that we wanted a hung jury or that we were sentenced on contempt charges while the jury was out, she would be "still in that deliberating room to this day." But she was certain then that a hung jury would result in the government's calling a new trial with possibly an even worse jury. And she believed that Judge Hoffman's continuous threats about contempt of court would result only in a "bawling out," not in jail sentences. She and her three allies finally became hysterical and collapsed under the pressure. Upon returning to the jury room after the reading of the verdicts, the four began weeping. "I went to pieces," Fritz recalled later. "I started to cry, and I couldn't stop. I kept saying over and over again, 'I just voted five men guilty on speeches I don't even remember.'"

It took Jean Fritz a month to recover physically. She also received bomb threats and hate mail for two years. "We're going to burn your house down if you don't move in a month" is the way she recalls a typical threat. Slowly she recovered. "It's just lucky I had a good family," she said. "My husband was wonderful."

The next day, February 20, we were brought back for sentencing and our final say. Dave reiterated that he would "sleep better and happier and with a greater sense of fulfillment in whatever jail I am in for the next however many years than if I had compromised, if I had sat here passively in the courthouse while justice was being throttled and the truth being denied." Rennie spoke ironically of his boy-next-door image, warning Foran that when he was released from prison he would move next door to him and convert his children. Abbie spoke of the portraits behind the judge. "I know those guys on the wall. I know them better than you. I played with Sam Adams on the Concord bridge. It was right near my home in Massachusetts. I was there when Paul Revere rode right up on his motorcycle and said, 'The pigs are coming, the pigs are coming.'" Then Abbie turned more emotional than I'd ever seen him:

> I don't even know what a riot is. I thought a riot was fun. I didn't want to be that serious. I was supposed to be funny. I tried to be, but it was sad last night in jail. I am not made out

to be a martyr. I tried to sign up for a few years, but when I went down there they ran out of nails. So what was I going to do? So I ended up being funny. But it wasn't funny last night sitting in a prison cell, a five-by-eight room, with no light and bedbugs all over. And it's fitting that if you went to the South and fought for voter registration and got arrested and beaten eleven or twelve times on those dusty roads for no bread, it's only fitting that you be arrested and tried under a "civil rights" act. That's the way it works.

Jerry Rubin held up a copy of his new book, published opportunely in time for the trial's end. Inside there was a picture of him as a clean young Cincinnati reporter. "I used to look like this, Judge, see," he said, holding up the volume.

Most everyone around this table once looked like this, and we all believed in the American system . . . . I'm being sentenced to five years, not for what I did in Chicago, but because some of us don't want to have a piece of the pie . . . . You are sentencing us for being ourselves. Because we don't look like this anymore. That's our crime.

Jerry then gave a copy of the book to the judge, with the inscription "Julius, you radicalized more young people than we ever could. You're the country's top Yippie."

For my last words I chose to speak as rationally as possible to Foran and the press, to underscore the futility of what the government was doing. Foran had commented that the verdict showed that "the system worked." I invited him to bring television cameras into Cook County jail to have the prisoners there comment on how the system was working. I tried to analyze the verdict as a perfect example of how a seemingly "democratic" system could actually be repressive. Foran had structured the indictment, I claimed, so that the jury could find some of the defendants innocent (Froines and Weiner) and find the rest of us guilty of one charge but not the other, thus achieving a "fair" conclusion. I asked Foran directly, "If you didn't want to make us martyrs, why did you do it? If you wanted to keep it cool, why didn't you give us a permit?" Finally I spoke of the jury, now departed:

> I feel sorry for the jury. I have a lot of sympathy for the jury that is similar to the sympathy I have for the older people of America who try their best to see through a network of lies . . . and go home each night with good consciences feeling they have done everything they could to help everybody all around . . . .
>
> The older people of America have tried their best to end the war in Vietnam. They have gone on record many times against the war in presidential primaries, in Gallup polls. And that should be enough in a democracy to prevent a war of massive aggression from going on. People try through the system to register their feelings, and then they go home to watch color TV, have oxtail soup and see their poodle, hoping that nobody blames them. Well, I don't blame them. I feel it is a tragedy, and in a tragedy you don't blame a person.
>
> In fact I feel that if a group of people the jury's age from this Chicago area could hear everything from the police and prosecutors they've told about us, and if four of them still believe we are innocent, I believe that is testimony of the ability of people to wake up, to wake up from the nightmare of American life. The tragedy is that people of that older generation do not yet know how to hold out, and probably never will, do not know how to fight to the end . . .
>
> I have no doubt—that if we had a jury of our peers, by any definition of the term "peers," we would have walked out of this place, or we would have had an absolutely hung jury because younger people in the country today know what prin-

ciples are. . . . and know how to stand up. . . . They are expressing their convictions now in the streets; our real jury is acquitting us now. But they do not have power yet.

They will have power. They will have power very soon. They will have the power to right the wrong that Len Weinglass spoke about. They will have the power to let us out of jail. They will have the power to see that this never happens again . . . . They are going to proclaim that imperative from the statehouse and from the courthouse. It's only a matter of time. You can give us time, and you are going to. But it's only a matter of time.

We went back to jail for another week, denied bail. While our lawyers appealed the judge's bail denial, we watched on prison television reruns of young people burning down the Bank of America in Santa Barbara. The media reported that a half million people went into the streets protesting the verdict. We said nothing. In prison everyone wears masks. We wondered if the burning and rioting would influence the higher courts to grant us bail, or whether it ensured our imprisonment as "dangerous men," the term Judge Hoffman used in denying our bail. We had a few visits from lawyers and friends, who could speak to us only through tiny, screened partitions on the other side of thick glass walls.

On February 28, the decision came from the Seventh Circuit Court of Appeals: we were granted bail. We were free again. We whooped and packed our books and clothing, then waited for the bail money to be raised, $25,000 per person. Somehow the amount that came spilling in to free us ran over the level needed by $17,000. We immediately and joyously turned it over to our fellow prisoners, bailing out nearly twenty of them with us.

In the days and weeks ahead, we learned significantly more about the jury that convicted us. The information was contained in copyrighted articles in the *Chicago Sun-Times* published by our early hope, juror Kay Richards, articles which were arranged, we learned, by her husband, Tom Stevens, whom Jean Fritz had correctly identified as a Daley man. Kay believed that "the trial had to come to some kind of conclusion just to prove that it works. It hurts people but it works." To fail to come to a verdict, in other words, would not be a triumph of individual conscience but further proof that the system was falling apart. Therefore, Kay described her attempts to put together a "compromise on punishment" between the eight jurors who favored conviction (including, she said, two who thought we should be shot) and the four who favored acquittal. The individual juror's judgment of whether the facts justified a guilty or not guilty verdict were beside the point in this effort to arrange a trade-off. "We couldn't understand the indictment. We didn't really know what the charges were," Kay wrote. Instead, they tended to divide into one faction of those that believed in stern punishment for rebellious kids and another, more permissive bloc.

"I think we just gave in," Jean Fritz said. "We were scared, and we had just given in." When she finally returned home, she said, "the whole street was filled with cameras."

When it was over, I called my mother in Oconomowoc, trying to cheer her up. "I think we'll win on appeal, Mom. Don't worry about it. The appeal takes a long time." She was hiding from reporters, having her mail forwarded from Michigan to where she was staying. In Wisconsin, she could get daily news coverage of the trial from the Chicago media. During the trial she called Anne in Berkeley a few times—a woman she didn't know in a place she'd never been—to get reports on my doings and interpretations of the trial's progress. She would close by making Anne promise to make me brush my teeth. Now that the verdict was in, I don't think she believed my breezy assurances.

In Detroit, my father closed the drapes in his house. He told his wife, Esther, an emotional and forgiving woman, of his fear that little Mary, my six-year-old sister, might be kidnapped. "No one should know who her brother is," he warned. I continued to write him, not expecting an answer. He would read the letters at the dining room table, and say nothing.

"Why don't you write to Tom, you bullheaded Irishman?" Esther would yell at him. "You know Tom and his friends are young. This is not our world anymore, and you've got to let them do what they want to do."

He never answered. Every night he watched the television news of the trial and pored over the Detroit papers. Once he turned to Esther and muttered about a "goddamned lie," advising her "don't believe what you read in the papers." Another time, speaking directly to the television set, he said, "My son is not a communist." When the trial ended, and the news coverage was over, he rose, as he did every night, and went into their bedroom without saying a word.

It was winter in America. The sixties were over.

AFTER THE TRIAL

The end of the Chicago trial was one of the many events that seemed to end the sixties. On February 20, 1970, five defendants were found guilty of incitement, but not guilty of conspiracy, convictions which carried a five-year sentence. Two defendants, Froines and Weiner, were cleared on both counts. Eight days later, the U.S. Seventh Circuit Court of Appeals rejected Judge Hoffman's denial of bail, and we were set free, on appeal, in an apparently unfree society.

On the day of our convictions, hundreds of campuses erupted in protests and riots. We watched on television from Cook County jail as young people burned down the Bank of America branch in Isla Vista.

The following month, on March 6, 1970, three members of the Weather Underground died in a New York townhouse when a bomb they were building accidentally exploded. I knew them all, as younger members who came from the embittered and revolutionary late-1960s generation of Students for a Democratic Society.

Then on April 30, Nixon invaded Cambodia, setting off a fierce national polarization. It happened that I was speaking at a Yale protest against the trial of Bobby Seale. When the news of Cambodia spread, the students gathered in New Haven called a national student strike that resulted in the shutdowns of hundreds of universities for the semester.

Three days later, on May 4, the Ohio National Guard shot and killed four innocent students at Kent State University, wounding nine others; ten days later, on May 15, two more students were killed by troopers at Jackson State. A presidential commission found that "the crisis on American campuses has no parallel in the history of this nation."

But even as our lives, and the life of the nation, seemed to teeter on the brink, a gathering storm of reform was welling up against Nixon and the war, symbolized in the Watergate crisis. Nixon's commitment to pursue an unpopular war led him to extra-constitutional and undemocratic suspensions of civil liberties and democratic processes, not only in his prosecution of the Chicago conspiracy, but in his pursuit of enemy lists and other repressive machinations. Instead of the civil war I was beginning to expect, America experienced a sudden surge of renewal.

The Senate hearings on the Watergate break-ins began in May, 1972. The peace and civil rights movements swept through the Democratic Party primaries that year to nominate George McGovern and rudely unseat the old guard of Cold War hawks. McGovern would not win in November, but the barriers to enfranchisement were breaking down. Eighteen-year-olds could vote and the military draft was terminated. The antiwar forces in Congress were rising, emboldened by huge May Day demonstrations in 1971, led by Rennie Davis, where 15,000 were detained in a Washington football stadium.

Even though such movement organizations as Students for a Democratic Society and the Student Nonviolent Coordinating Committee were gone, and even though our leaders were assassinated, the peace, justice and environmental movements continued growing to peak levels, almost spontaneously.

By August 1974, the movements had prevailed as Nixon was driven from office and Congress steadily terminated funding for the wars in Indochina.

In the same hopeful period—or perhaps because of it—the fortunes of the Chicago conspirators improved as well. Bobby Seale and his codefendants were acquitted in New Haven. On November 21, 1972, the Seventh Circuit reversed our convictions. The same federal court had reversed our contempt citations on May 11 of the same year, but the prosecutors insisted on a retrial of all 154 citations, beginning in September 1973, as the Nixon era drew to its ignominious close. A new federal judge threw out 146 of those contempt citations on December 5, 1973, finding Kunstler, Dellinger, Rubin and Hoffman guilty of fourteen. The judge credited those defendants with time served, and so we all walked away, free at last, on that freezing December day.

As we left the Chicago courtroom for the last time, I carried in my arms my six-month-old son Troy, my child with Jane Fonda. For that brief and unexpected moment, everything seemed possible.

ABOUT THE AUTHORS

TOM HAYDEN is a prolific writer. He has written from jails, jungles, Harvard offices and from a legislative chamber. He has authored fifteen books and hundreds of op-ed articles and essays. These days, Hayden writes regularly for the *Nation*, where he is a member of the editorial board. He blogs continually for the *Huffington Post*. As he was obsessed with ending the Vietnam War forty years ago, Hayden now spends his time helping to end the war in Iraq, writing, teaching a class, interviewing Iraqis, and serving as an adviser to America's leading anti-war coalitions. As he was engaged in the civil rights movement decades ago, today Hayden is an engaged witness to labor and human rights movements against corporate globalization. And as he pondered the deeper issues when he wrote the *Port Huron Statement* in 1961, Hayden still writes about the importance of social movements like few others. He brings a combination of experiences in community organizing, resistance against authority, serving as a populist state senator, and teaching in universities that make him rare and unique.

Hayden entered the University of Michigan in time to be touched by the Southern student civil rights movement, the John F. Kennedy campaign, and the Peace Corps. He was chosen editor of the *Michigan Daily*, but passed up a journalism career to work on the front lines of the civil rights movement. He was a Freedom Rider in southern Georgia in 1961, and wrote blazing dispatches for national audiences, including *Mademoiselle* magazine. He drafted what became the *Port*

Huron Statement from an Albany, Georgia, jail cell in late 1961. The document became the founding manifesto of the Students for a Democratic Society, and has been hailed as the greatest document of the New Left era.

Hayden left university life to become a community organizer in the Newark ghetto, 1964–68. When Vietnam was bombed and invaded starting in 1965, however, Hayden began opposing the war as a derailment of the fight for social justice in America. He was an early traveler to Hanoi and opponent of the war and draft. His opposition to Vietnam led Hayden to participate in the Columbia student strike in April 1968 and the militant street protests in Chicago that same year. He was indicted with seven others by the Nixon administration, convicted in 1969, and acquitted on appeal in 1973. He was married at the time to actress Jane Fonda, with whom he has a son and stepdaughter.

After the war, Hayden entered California politics for two decades, winning seven out of eleven races, and chairing legislative policy committees on natural resources, higher education and labor. He authored over 100 measures that became law, and was described as "the conscience of the Senate" when he retired in 2000.

Hayden continues to write prolifically, and has taught in recent years at Pitzer College, Occidental College, and the Harvard Institute of Politics. His most recent books are *Street Wars* (2005), *The Lost Gospel of the Earth* (2005), *The Port Huron Statement* (2006), *Ending the War in Iraq* (2006) and *Writings for a Democratic Society: The Tom Hayden Reader* (2008). His Web site is www.tomhayden.com.

RON SOSSI, artistic director/founder of the Odyssey Theatre Ensemble in Los Angeles, received a BA in Theatre from the University of Michigan where he won the Avery Hopwood Playwriting Award, and an MA in Film from UCLA, where he was awarded the Samuel Goldwyn Creative Writing Award. He served hard time as an executive in film and TV at the Mirisch Corporation, ABC Television, Paramount

Studios and Metromedia. In these jobs he was in charge of such tele-vision shows as *Bewitched, The Flying Nun, Mission Impossible, Big Valley, The Young Lawyers,* and *The Odd Couple,* was a credited TV writer and director, and developed/packaged a number of television movies.

Not happy with the "industry" and initially as a frustration outlet, Sossi founded the Odyssey Theatre Ensemble in 1969. In 1973 he moved the theater to a larger building in West Los Angeles and left the film industry to devote himself fully to the development of an experimental and internationally oriented theater. He's worked with and been influenced by the ideas of Jerzy Grotowski in Poland, Peter Brook in England, and Joseph Chaikin in New York, as well as the seminal work of Michael Chekhov and Bertolt Brecht. In addition to numerous directing/producing awards, Sossi was awarded the Los Angeles Drama Critics Circle's prestigious Margaret Harford Award, for "demonstrating a continual willingness to experiment provoca-tively in the process of theatre" and in 1999 the first LADCC Award for lifetime achievement in directing. He has served on the boards of Theatre LA, Theatre Communications Group, the Mayor's Bicenten-nial Committee, Olympic Arts Festival Theatre Committee and the Policy Panel of the National Endowment for the Arts. He has been a panelist for the California Arts Council and the N.E.A. As a guest fac-ulty member, Sossi has taught at UCLA, UC San Diego, Cal Arts, Pomona College, LA City College, Whittier College, Cal State Fuller-ton, American Academy of Dramatic Arts, and USC, and currently teaches courses in directing and acting at Loyola Marymount. As a State Department–sponsored director, he helmed the Finnish pre-miere of *M. Butterfly.* The 2001 recipient of the Durfee Foundation Award, Sossi made a sabbatical trip to India to research aspects of Hindu and Buddhist ritual for *Buddha's Big Nite,* a 2002 process piece developed with the Koan group, a body of eight actors within the Odyssey Theatre umbrella, developing a yearly original work along experimental lines. Among his many award-winning productions are

Peer Gynt, The Chicago Conspiracy Trial, Threepenny Opera, Edmond (Olympic Arts Festival offering), Master Class, Mary Barnes, Idioglossia (turned into the Jodie Foster film Nell), Far Away, Taking Sides, The Greeks (named 2000 Production of the Year by LA Weekly), and such Koan-created works as Faust Projekt, Kafka Thing, Buddha's Big Nite and Sliding Into Hades, which captured the major 2007 L. A. Weekly Awards for Production of the Year, Best Director (Sossi) and Best Production Design. Sossi has produced/directed most of the works of Bertolt Brecht.

As a producer, Sossi is also a winner of a Cable Ace Award in 1987 for Outstanding Dramatic Production for the HBO special based upon the work contained herein.

FRANK CONDON has directed all five of the professional productions of The Chicago Conspiracy Trial to date, including the original production at the Odyssey Theatre in Los Angeles. That production garnered him Los Angeles Drama Critic's Circle Awards for both directing and playwriting. He has received a National Endowment for the Arts Director's Fellowship, and he was granted the Mayor and County Supervisors' Fellowship Award by the Sacramento (CA) Metropolitan Arts Commission for "a lifetime contribution to the field on a national level." Frank was invited by Luis Valdez to direct the first play in El Teatro Campesino's home theater in San Juan Bautista, California. He has directed several highly regarded original plays, several of which were subsequently produced around the country. He worked with Gary (Doonesbury) Trudeau on the continually updated and highly successful runs of Trudeau's musical revue Rap Master Ronnie, which he directed in Los Angeles, San Diego, San Francisco, Seattle, and Toronto. Frank also directed the original production of Mark Medoff's The Majestic Kid at the Denver Center Theatre Company. The professional schools with which he has been affiliated include the American Academy of Dramatic Arts and the Dell'Arte School of Comedy. He was a visiting associate professor at UCLA, and a guest artist/professor at USC, UCSD, and other major colleges and universities. Frank is the founding artistic director of River Stage in Sacramento, California. He is a member of the Society of Stage Directors and Choreographers, and a member of the Dramatists Guild.

Allen Ginsberg and William Burroughs, Chicago, 1968. MICHAEL COOPER

CITY LIGHTS PUBLICATIONS
www.citylights.com

ISBN PREFIX: 978-0-87286

Wilson, Peter Lamborn. SACRED DRIFT: Essays on the Margins of Islam (275-5)
Wolverton, Terry. INSURGENT MUSE: Life & Art at the Woman's Building (403-0)
Zamora, Daisy. RIVERBED OF MEMORY Pocket Poets #49 (273-9)
Zinn, Howard. A POWER GOVERNMENTS CANNOT SUPPRESS (475-8)

CITY LIGHTS FOUNDATION BOOKS (ISBN prefix: 978-1-931404)

Carlsson, Chris, ed. THE POLITICAL EDGE (05-4)
Ferlinghetti, Lawrence. SAN FRANCISCO POEMS Poet Laureate Series #1 (01-1)
Frank, Dana. LOCAL GIRL MAKES HISTORY: Exploring Northern California's Kitsch
    Monuments (09-7)
Gray-Garcia, Lisa. CRIMINAL OF POVERTY: Growing Up Homeless in America (07-5)
Hirschman, Jack. ALL THAT'S LEFT (08-2)
Major, Devorah, ed. THE OTHER SIDE OF THE POSTCARD (06-2)
Major, Devorah. WHERE RIVER MEETS OCEAN Poet Laureate Series #3 (03-8)
Mirikitani, Janice. LOVE WORKS Poet Laureate Series #2 (02-x)
Myrick, David. SAN FRANCISCO'S TELEGRAPH HILL cloth (00-3)